Toe Boys
GROWING UP

DR. LACEY COLTER, SR.
"CODAS"

PublishAmerica
Baltimore

First printing

ISBN: 1-4137-8334-1
PUBLISHED BY PUBLISHAMERICA, LLLP
www.publishamerica.com
Baltimore

Printed in the United States of America

Dedication

It is with great love, respect, honor and appreciation that I dedicate this book to my sister Lillie Lou Colter-Tabb, who is now present with the Lord. She was my biggest fan, and was there for me when I needed family the most.

I also dedicate this book to the mothers of Rillito, Arizona. Thank you for loving us unconditionally and for teaching us to love each other. You made the Toe an example of a village raising a child. I thank each mother for begetting all of us in love and raising all of us as your children. It is written, "Spare the rod and you spoil the child." We thank you for not sparing the rod and for not spoiling us. We learned that discipline when administered in love is a very powerful tool.

Thank you for allowing us to be children for as long as we could, but now we are men. It is written, "*When I was a child I spoke as a child, I understood as a child, I thought as a child, but when I became a man I put away childish things*" (1Corinthians 13:11, KJV).

Table of Contents

CHAPTER ONE

The Beginning

I was born at a time when men were men and women were women, and there were no in between. A time when good was the opposite of evil and love was more than just a word, but an action. A time when law was order and beauty was more than skin deep, because it came from a person's heart. A time when there were differences between adults and children and when one God prevailed over all things. It was a good time to grow up and growing up is what we did.

I was born in Crockett, Texas, and I am told it was named after Davy Crockett. At the age of six months old, my parents came to Arizona by way of New Mexico. Our family was very poor and being Black made things even worse. My mother had just lost a child, and after trying again, I was born. I was the youngest of eleven children.

I don't know much about the journey or the reason we left Texas; perhaps it was to find cotton fields with more cotton and higher wages, but somewhere along the way we landed in Continental, Arizona. We lived, of course, on the other side of the tracks with other Black and Native American families. My dad was a farmhand and my mother normally worked in the fields. I can actually remember lying on the end of her cotton sack and sleeping as my mother picked cotton and pulled me along. I could feel the leaves from the stalks reaching out and brushing me lightly along the length of my body. The smell of cotton and dirt, and the bristling of the leaves, were the perfect combination to promote good sleep.

Sometimes my older sister would care for us at the car while they worked. They would park the car at the end of the cotton rows and come and see about us whenever they weighed their cotton sacks, if they were picking cotton, or when they had chopped to the end of their row when they were chopping cotton.

I learned many lessons while in this small community, and one of them was that death is inevitable. I learned that if you die in Christ, this earth is the only hell you have to worry about, but if you die out of the will of Christ, then this is your only heaven.

I have learned that if you live long enough adversity is unavoidable, and anyone God takes from this earth can never be replaced. The void they leave can be filled, but no one can be replaced.

The greatest irreversible tragedy is the lost of a loved one or a family member. The first of such loses occurred prior to my illness, which came from an outbreak of typhoid.

My sister Bernie (Bernice) was called by the Death Angel. I believe that everyone, prior to death, hears the call of the Death Angel or the Angel of Death. Few people listen and know that the end is near, while others know, but they refuse to listen. When the Death Angel calls, people do the strangest things in preparation after that calling. Some people clean up their homes, or do clean up details in their lives. Some have financial layouts prepared. They give away things that you never thought they would. The most precious and cherished possessions are passed on to others simply because the Death Angel knocked on life's door and they listened. It is very mysterious, the reactions of individuals who know they are going to die. If you have ever been around someone who heard the Death Angel and died, in retrospect, you can recall things they said and did to remind you that they knew their time was winding up.

Bernie was seventeen years old, and she was a very beautiful girl just beginning her life and full of hope. She had a big smile and wore glasses that seemed a bit large for her thin face. Sometimes the glasses slid down to the tip of her nose and rested there. Often she would gaze over them like a college professor. She had long Black hair that extended farther when she straightened it with the old-fashioned straightening combs. Bernice was of a fair complexion and had a sponge for a heart. It seemed she absorbed everyone's feelings, and it made her very empathetic. She was just married and had a six-month-old son.

One day the Death Angel spoke to Bernie and she began acting very strange.

She would answer aloud, "Yes, what do you want…who called?"

She would question us to see if we had called her name, but we never called her nor did we know what she was talking about.

She would say, "Somebody called my name, Bernice, Bernice, didn't y'all hear?"

She would start taking long walks along the railroad tracks of Continental, Arizona, searching for the voice. She was determined to find the person. Every day she would walk and search for the voice, but to no avail. She could never find it or its source. Then one day I heard Bernie talking to Mama.

She said, "Mama, something is wrong."

"In what way, baby?" Mama asked.

"I keep hearing someone call my name, but when I go looking, ain't nobody there."

I saw Mama look at Bernie with concern and she replied, "Next time you hear the voice, say what do you want Lord?"

The next day Bernie went walking again, but this time it was different. When she returned, she told Mama what happened.

"Mama," said Bernie, "I asked like you said and I think I know what I must do. I've got to go away, Mama, but I don't want to leave you and the baby. Mama, I don't want to go so soon."

I saw, for the first time in my life, tears in mama's eyes, but I didn't know why. Then Bernie said to Mama, as Mama was lightly touching her hair and holding her in her arms, "Mama, it's gonna be all right, it's gonna be all right." She took Mama's hand from off her head and kissed it several times.

I thought to myself, *Where is Bernice going that makes her so sad?* I later learned that Bernie wasn't sad about where she was going, but because she had to leave so soon.

I am reminded of the story in the Bible (1 Samuel, Chapter 3): Samuel was just a child when he first heard a voice from God speaking to him. Samuel would get up and go to Eli and say, *"Here am I."* Eli would tell

Samuel to go and lie down. He had no idea what Samuel was talking about. After the third time Eli perceived that the Lord had called the child and told him to respond by saying, *"Speak Lord; for thy servant heareth."* Samuel did so and God spoke to him. This reminds me of what Bernie was going through with the Death Angel.

Later that day, Bernie was at home with her six-month-old son, my sister Mary and myself; we were eight and three years old respectively. We watched Bernie as she played with her child, little Frankie, and talked with us. Little did we know that the Death Angel had spoken for the last time. At the age of three, I can vividly recall the events of that tragic day. It is like a movie that continually plays in my mind, and I can never forget.

A loud voice shouted, "Hey!"

When we turned, we could see her husband Frank standing in the doorway. Frank had been hanging around with some of the adults who meant him no good. He was young and gullible, and he drank too much. His older brother was married to my mother's younger sister. It was a strange connection, but there wasn't any kindred blood shared.

When Frank came home that day from drinking and listening to his friends, he was intoxicated and possessed with evil intent. He was in a rage, swearing and grabbing and throwing things. It seemed from nowhere he brandished a weapon—a handgun—and pointed it at her, and he threatened to kill her. She reminded him that there were children in the room and he should clean up his language and put the gun away.

"You don't think I'll shoot you, bitch?" he blurted through his slurred speech.

His eyes were red as an evening blaze and sweat dripped from his forehead. It was as if Satan himself had sent him on a mission and nothing would stop him from carrying it out.

I heard Bernie pleading with him to put the gun down. I have never known why he was in such a rage, but it did appear he was acting out of jealousy. He cursed and planted himself in the doorway to try and block our exit. He pointed the weapon at Bernie, who was holding the baby, and again threatened to kill her. There was a split moment of silence, and then he fired twice, POW! POW! The sound was deafening and frightening; my sister Mary and I screamed with terror. Bernie felt the impact of both bullets as they tore into her upper body. One bullet entered through her armpit, because she was turned sideways while holding the baby, and it exited her chest, hitting the child. The bullet grazed little Frankie, tearing away the top of his navel. The baby started screaming with pain, due to the heat of the bullet severing part of his navel, and the sudden blast from the weapon frightened him. The blood sprayed from his wound. Bernie was knocked backwards by the impact of the shots and was covered with blood, but she did not drop the baby. She laid the baby on the bed and staggered pass Frank, who was standing sideways in the doorway. He allowed her to brush pass him in the doorway, leaving bloodstains on his clothing. The blood began to saturate her clothing as it gushed forth like a dam that had burst to release its waters.

Frank (Chinch) was standing there holding the gun as if it was a stranger to him. The gunshots seemed to awaken him to a point of sobriety. He looked as though he was asking himself, *What just happened? How did this weapon get into my hands?*

Bernie staggered passed him, never looking at him at all, but having her mind fixed on her destination, as she tried desperately to reach our parents, who were in the barracks next door.

I passed by him in the doorway, but I didn't think about being shot. I only wanted to follow my sister who was hurt and fighting for her life. I followed her as she slowly went to the barracks next door to where Mom and Dad were talking about the day's events. They, too, had become concerned about the noise they had just heard. The last thing on their mind was the tragedy that had just unfolded.

"Mama, Mama," she cried, as she stumbled along. It took all her strength to make it next door to the attached barrack. With every ounce of her life oozing out of her body, she fell against the screen door, and using every bit of her strength, she was barely able to turn the knob and open the door. Slowly she staggered inside. Everything she touched was scarlet red with her blood, which profusely poured from her body like a fountain. There were bloodstains on everything she touched. Her clothes were soaked with blood. It was devastating watching the essence of life flow from her open wounds. As she would lift her feet slowly to take the next step, her footprint in the dirt would quickly fill with blood and a watery liquid. This was an indication that the bullets had pierced her heart. The steps that Bernie took to get to Mama's arms were outlined in crimson.

The imprint of her every step contained drops of Bernie's life being left behind on the ground. Her blood cried out from the ground for God to give her strength to make it to Mama's arms.

My father was sitting in a chair watching Bernie as she entered the room, but was frozen and speechless from peering at the gruesome sight. Bernie was covered with blood that had soaked through her clothes and had run the length of her arms and was dripping from her fingertips. She leaned backwards against the wall for support as she made her way towards my father. Finally, with no more strength, she slid down the wall to her knees and fell forward across my father's lap. Daddy sat in total disbelief and he was speechless as he touched Bernie, and then lifted up his hands to examine the red coloring. She was crying softly, but in a soft and weak voice she spoke to Mama who was across the room.

"Mama, I've been shot," she whispered softly. "Mama, I've been shot."

Mama ran from across the room to where Bernie was lying crouched over Daddy's lap. The reality of Bernie's pain was in plain view and Mama's heart broke as she reached for her child.

Dad sat there petrified and in shock, and the tears begin flowing from his eyes like rivers of water as he begin to perceive the reality of the situation. Mama ran to Bernie, lifting her up into her arms, and they both fell against the wall. They were pressed against the wall as Bernie again slid down the wall, still in Mama's arms.

I heard my mother say, "No God, not my baby, please God, not my baby, my baby!"

Bernie lay there in Mama's arms—the loving arms that had held her many times and had not failed to ever comfort her. The arms that had held her so gentle and for so many years as a child, and were now holding her unto death. Just a few days earlier she had rested in those same arms as she told Mama about the voice of the Death Angel. Yes, even unto death Mama's arms comforted Bernice. They both sat on the floor in each other's arms, covered in the scarlet essence of life that drained from her. Tears were flowing softly and both hearts beating together.

For one last time, Bernice looked into the tear-stained face of a grieving mother, about to lose the whole world, and she said softly, "Mama, I've been shot. It's gonna be all right, Mama, it's gonna be all right."

Then I heard Mama plead to God one last time for the life of her child, "No God, please, not my baby, my baby!"

Bernie continued to gaze into a grieving face and into the eyes of a mother that were cloudy with tears. She whispered, "Mama, it's okay. I'm going home."

Both of their hearts beat frantically and then one slowed until there was only one heart beating among the arms that were entangled in an embrace. Bernice closed her eyes and her heart ceased to beat.

I believe for a brief moment Mama's heart stopped also. She died with Bernie for a little while. Bernie's body grew limp and she appeared relaxed for the first time since she heard the call of the Death Angel. It seemed she was at such great peace and appeared so comfortable there in Mama's arms.

The voice she now heard was that of the heavenly choir singing softly as she made her entrance through the gates of pearls and into the presence of God. Her spirit was now free, and she went home to be with the Lord. For it is written, "*to be absent from the body, is to be present with the Lord*" (2 Corinthians 5:8, KJV).

She went to a place where we are told will be of many mansions.

Christ said, "*Let not your heart be troubled: ye believe in God, believe also in me. In my Father's house are many mansions: if it were not so, I would have told you. I go to prepare a place for you. And if I go and prepare a place for you, I will come again and receive you unto myself that where I am, there ye may be also. And whither I go ye know, and the way ye know*" (John 14:1-4, KJV).

This is the place where she would no longer have to hear the voice of the Death Angel. Yes, that day Bernie's spirit, "*returned to God whom gave it*" (Ecclesiastes 12:7, KJV).

Frank was still in the apartment gazing at the weapon when reality hit him like a bolt of lightning. He fell to his knees and cried with a loud voice, "Oh my God, I done shot my wife! I done killed my wife!" He dropped the weapon, and with his face in his hands, he wept hysterically.

The police came and took him away. After they had all left, I followed my older brother Willie, as he walked to the screen door, and observed through tearful eyes the blood of our sister covering the door post. He retrieved a pocket knife from his front pocket and started trimming the wood that was covered with blood. I watched him as he cried in silence and made a futile empty to erase the evidence of what had happened. Perhaps, hoping that by removing the blood, he could erase what had occurred.

I thought God was so cruel not to answer Mama. I saw her sitting there drenched in the blood of her loving child, asking God not to take her baby. I knew then that God did not answer my mother's prayer.

A few days later we had Bernie's home-going (Christian funeral), and I told my mother that I didn't love God anymore, because he didn't answer her prayer. I was surprised when she turned to me with tearful eyes and sat me down before her.

"Son, don't ever say that you don't love God on account of me," said Mama. "God does answer prayers, and He did answer my prayer. Sometimes we have to wait for that answer; sometimes the answer comes immediately, sometimes the answer is yes, and sometimes the answer is no. Don't ever forget that when death knocks we all must answer."

This incident remains a mystery today: where did Frank get the gun? What was he upset about? Who was he drinking with that day? All these things did come out in court, but I was too young to remember. I was told later in life that the gun belonged to my Uncle Sly. My sister Mary testified against Frank and did an excellent job for an eight-year-old. Frank was convicted of first-degree murder and was sentenced to life in prison. His only defense was, "I was drunk." The sentence was surprising, because in those days Black-on-Black crime was ignored in most parts of the country.

CHAPTER TWO

Big Red

There is a saying: "when it rain, it pours." Symbolically, adversity is something that has a tendency to pour. It's like Murphy's Law, if it can get worse it will.

Two years later there was an epidemic of rabies throughout the camp. Many of the domestic animals had become infected by coyotes, skunks and other wild animals.

We children were playing in the yard when my dog, Big Red, came from the woods acting very strange. He was a large dog with red hair and a strong body. He was a mutt and mixed with every kind of dog that wandered the campsite, but he was my best friend. He was growling at everyone and acting as if he didn't know anyone. He had been gone for a few days, so I thought he was out chasing some female in heat. His peculiar behavior made me think he was just getting old and grumpy. He was foaming at the mouth and was staggering against walls, stumbling over broken chairs and seemed down right mad at everyone. Many of the kids were afraid and ran inside their houses. I wasn't really paying much attention to the children, because my eyes were on my buddy, Big Red. I looked around and noticed that I was the only one outside. Big Red started running circles around the barracks as if he was disoriented. I thought to myself, *This is enough!* If we were going to have some fun I'd better catch him and tie him up. As he came around the corner I approached him, and got right in the path of Big Red, so I could stop him. I was tired of this mess.

Suddenly, I felt something come over me, and I stopped in my tracks. Something was really wrong with him. I sensed something evil about the look on his face as he approached me. He was blind with madness, and he didn't seem to know me. He was gritting his teeth and coming straight towards me. I knew he was blind with rage, and that I could become his victim. I begin slowly backing away. He began to cut the distance between us. Every step seemed to get shorter and Big Red was getting closer and closer. I could sense I was close to the house, but I was afraid to turn around. As I took a step backwards, I fell. Big Red leaped at me, but just as he leaped I kicked and hit Big Red in the mouth. He bit the heel of my shoe, taking it off my foot and shaking it in his mouth like a shark that had bitten his prey. He rolled like an alligator doing a death roll with its prey trapped in its jaws. He was tearing it to threads as he growled, snarled and chewed. I continued crawling backwards, trying to spread the distance between Big Red and myself. Then the reality of me not being in the shoe struck him. He shook his head one final time, throwing the shoe several feet away. He turned and with all the hatred and wrath of an animal possessed with the intent to kill, he started after me. I was paralyzed with fear.

A thousand thoughts flashed through my mind, but one thought stood out above all. Wait a minute. Why hadn't I heard the voice of the Death Angel? I lay there staring at Big Red about to make his final charge. I saw him leave the ground, all four paws flying through the air, his foaming mouth wide open and aimed for my throat. He was about three feet away and we were face to face as he soared through the air. Suddenly, there was a sound like thunder that comes with a flash of lightning. An unknown force hit Big Red and knocked him down to the ground beside me. I heard him cry out in pain, and I thought, *What happened?* The impact had knocked him out of mid-air and onto the ground beside me. I saw him lying there covered in blood. He gasped frantically for air but could get none. His chest expanded then he exhaled and became motionless by my side. Before he died I looked in his eyes, and I could sense, as he gained a moment of sanity, his plea for forgiveness.

I heard footsteps and I heard *thump-thump*! I turned and saw two empty shotgun shells on the ground beside me, and I heard a voice; oh, what a voice.

"You all right, son?" said a familiar voice.

I looked up from the position of lying on my back. Dad was looking down with tearful eyes, holding on to his double barrel shotgun, and both barrels were still smoking.

Big Red was lying there motionless. My emotions were mixed with both gratitude and sorrow. Oh, what a friend to have gone in such a manner.

"Big Red was a good dog, he didn't mean you no harm," Dad said. "He got rabies and he wasn't himself. He was no longer in control of his mind."

He paused for a moment, wiping his eyes with an old handkerchief and saying as he stuck it back into his coveralls, "I know you loved him, but he was about to attack someone that I love, and I couldn't let that happen. If there is a choice between you and Big Red, you are my choice."

Dad lifted me up from the ground and said, "I want you to remember Big Red the way he was before he got sick, and before all this happened."

My dad told me that many people remember others in their agony at the last moment of their lives prior to death, when they are not really themselves.

He reminded me, "Don't remember Big Red like that."

When I remember Big Red I think about what my father told me that day, and I remember a friend. I remember when I would ride him like a horse, and I used him like a pillow when I slept. When we would go chasing lizards and birds, I would throw rocks at the birds and every once in a while get lucky and hit one. They would fall out of the trees or flutter on the ground, and Big Red would beat me to them and claim them for himself. He would deny that I had done anything. He did prove his loyalty many times and attempted to give his life for me when he thought other dogs were trying to attack me. He would even growl at my friends when he thought they were too rough in their playing with me. We were inseparable and he was indeed my best friend. When I think of that tragic day, I think of it as the day my best friend died.

CHAPTER THREE

Faith Is the Answer

As a small child, five years old, I was stricken with a disease called typhoid (this was the illness mentioned earlier). In fact, I brought typhoid to our community and singlehandedly was responsible for all the outhouses in the community being demolished and replaced with more sanitized restrooms. I did learn one thing and that is "faith is the answer."

My friends and I would chase lizards, chickens and other things that had a way of getting the attention of a child. We would chase these animals and creatures into the oddest places. The White kids would have treehouses and some abandoned building to play in, but not us Black kids. We played in and around outhouses that had at one time been filled with human feces—defecation that had been covered with dirt and lime and had become so hard you could walk on it like a cement sidewalk. Now, you can only walk on crap for so long before you get infected with a disease and with me it was typhoid.

I was hospitalized, and as a result of the diagnosis, all the outhouses in the community of Continental, Arizona, had to be destroyed and replaced. They even sanitized and modernized them and made them flush.

Well, the hospital said I was about to "bite the dust" and that my parents may as well come and take me home to die. Of course, they didn't tell me that I had only two weeks to live. When Mom came in crying and

Dad shaking his head with that look on his face, I knew something was wrong. I thought their reaction was for my sister Mary, who had been admitted along with me. I thought she was the one not going to make it, but little did I know the verdict was against me.

It was immediately afterwards strange things started to happen. I was actually going to be sent home that day on a bus that ran through the area of Continental, but Mom and Dad had second thoughts about me riding the bus home, so they came and got me. I was in pretty bad shape. I couldn't walk, I couldn't hear very well and the disease had made me so weak I couldn't even care for myself. I was told I was going home that day and was supposed to ride the bus home, but in my condition, no way! I was so weak that catching a bus and getting off a quarter mile from the house would have posed a serious problem. A quarter of a mile is a long way to crawl.

Of course, they wouldn't tell me I was never expected to walk again and was expected to die within two weeks. Anyway, that's water under the bridge, because my parents came and picked me up, and we all started home to prepare for my demise. We traveled down the same road the bus went and saw the bus that I was supposed to be on involved in a fatal accident. It had run head-on into a motorcycle, burst into flames and many were killed. That was when I begin to sense that there was divine intervention being worked in my life.

We got home, and I didn't even have crutches. Of course, if I were White they would have given me a wheelchair with a motor and a cup holder for lemonade. I couldn't play with other kids because I couldn't walk, so I made my own wheelchair. With a creative and innovative mind I decided that I was going to become mobile. I took an old wagon, knocked a hole through the center of the floor and I stuck a rod through the hole to the ground. By this brilliant ingenuity I was able to pry myself along. Man, what an idea.

Another strange thing happened. Mama took me to a revival to be prayed for and the evangelist said I was chosen, like John the Baptist or Moses. Can you believe that? I was handpicked by God to be special. No way!

The evangelist just put his hands on me and said, "Lord, thou hast chosen this child," then he prayed a very strange prayer, "Lord, I have lived a good and long life, but this child has just begun to live. If death must come, let it be me and not him. Let this child live that he may fulfill your purpose in his life."

So it was said, so it was done. I don't know who this guy was trying to impress, but you don't play with God. Of course, there was a chance he was very sincere. The evangelist died and soon afterward I made a miraculous recovery. What a miracle!

One thing I learned from this is, be careful how you pray and what you say. You must make sure you are willing to deal with the consequences of your request. God will hear your persistent plea and give you what you ask for, but not to harm you or destroy you, but for your own personal reproof.

The Bible tells us, "*Those whom he loves he chastens.*" We continue to ask God for those things, which are detrimental to us, so God gives us a taste, so that we may see for ourselves. The Bible tells us that the children of Israel desired a king even after God told them that He was the only King they needed. They were persistent about the fact that they wanted to be like others who had a king. God warned them and then gave them a king for their chastisement. He gave them Saul (1Samuel Chapter 8).

The Bible tells us that God does not give us things that will destroy us. Matthew states, "*For every one that asketh receiveth; and he that seeketh findeth; and to him that knocketh it shall be opened. Or what man is there of you, whom if his son ask bread, will he give him a stone? Or if he asks for a fish, will he give him a serpent? If ye then, being evil, know how to give good gifts unto your children, how much more shall your Father which is in heaven give good things to them that ask him?*" (Matthew: 7:8-11, KJV).

While in this state of affliction I learned a lot about the mind of a child. Isn't it amazing that as a child you can do the most daring tasks simply because you don't know any better? One thing I believe is that child psychology makes sense to a child. For example, a child thinks like this: if you don't know certain things, then it is impossible to be hurt from lack of knowledge. It is when you know things that you get hurt. What I am saying is this, we are capable of doing the impossible until we find out what we did is impossible to do. When we become aware that it is impossible then it becomes impossible.

For example, as a kid we did things that would be considered impossible and fatal by an adult. We rode our bicycles with our eyes shut and no hands to see how far we could ride or how far we could go before we hit something. When our parents told us not to do that or we would get hurt, sure enough, we got hurt the next time we tried it. If they had not said anything, then nothing would have happened. Only when we were warned that something would happen, it happened.

We can eat certain things and touch things that are forbidden and nothing happens, until our parents tell us not to touch or eat it because it will kill us. Now before you got this information you could do it and live, but if you did it after you were told not to, there is no doubt you would fall over dead instantly. If you don't know it's harmful, then nothing happens, but when you learn the truth it will kill you. Now that's child psychology.

Sometimes people who are deathly sick live normal lives because they don't know they should have died last year. But as soon as the doctors tell them, give or take a month, they lose their will to live and sure enough they die. We are talking about death within a few days or, in some cases, a few hours. Some people go to the doctor feeling great, but when they find out from the doctor that they are deathly sick, they stop feeling great and become miserable until they die.

I didn't get sick until my parents said, "If you don't stop playing around them nasty outhouses, you're gonna get sick!"

Now try to picture this: scientists say that the structure of the bumblebee's wings in reference to the bee's body weight make it impossible for the bumblebee to fly. The wing structure is insufficient for lifting the weight of the bee. Can you believe that? The problem is this: no one has found a way to tell the bumblebee that he can't fly and because he doesn't know, that little sucker just keeps on flying. Believe me, as soon as science finds a way they are going to explain it to the bumblebee and every one of them bees are going to stop flying.

Can you imagine bees falling out the air all over the world once they get the news? Then as time passes them by, they will all be sitting around on the ground saying, "Wow, I remember when we used to fly, and then they told us that we couldn't, what a shame!"

As for my miraculous recovery, I later learned that it was not because I didn't know I was supposed to die that helped me to live, but because of the grace and mercy of an Almighty God. It was God that made it possible for me to walk the path He had chosen for me. I don't believe in luck, but I do believe that God allows the "*sun to rise on the evil and on the good, and sendeth rain on the just and on the unjust*" (Matthew 5:45, KJV). Little did I know that all of this was for a purpose.

At the age of six, I recovered and we were once again a total family. I was able to walk with legs they said I would never be able to stand on. I was able to hear out of a deaf ear they said could never hear sound and, of course, I went beyond the two weeks they gave me to live. God brought about a change in my life, and from that time to now, I never took His grace and mercy for granted.

CHAPTER FOUR

The Legend Begins

Dad was still cursing, drinking, gambling and taking care of his family. Mom was still praying, serving God and holding on to His unchanging hand. The hands we knew and had confidence would protect and guide us throughout our lives.

I learned that God is the same yesterday, today and forever, and faith in God is the answer to all things. The Bible tells us that "*God hath dealt to every man the measure of faith*" (Romans 12:3). We must understand that it is the source of your faith that is important. Christ should be the source of your faith, not riches or fame, silver and gold, or house and land.

My dad was about six feet three inches tall, skinny as a beanpole and balding. I heard he had red hair before it fell out and what was left turned grayish. He was in his early fifties and Mom was forty-three years old when I was born.

Dad had a sense of humor and believed in the existence of God. He believed in the various concepts of divinity, as far as God being the creator and being alive. Dad believed in the "check and balance system." Dad's concept was simply this: God judges a person by the goodness of his heart; or if that person does more good than bad, he had it made. Dad felt that if you were a good person doing good things, that was all that really counted. In retrospect, I wished I had known then what I know today. I could have told Dad that was not the way of salvation. Only through faith in Jesus

Christ is man saved. Not through your goodness or through your deeds. I am reminded of the scripture that says, "...*But we are all as an unclean thing and all our righteousness are as filthy rags; and we all do fade as a leaf; and our iniquities like the wind have taken us away*" (Isaiah 64:6, KJV). The good and righteous deeds we do outside of salvation are like filthy rags in the sight of God. Without Christ in your life, these things are in vain. Only through Christ are we able to make it through the doorway to eternal life. Doing good things and expecting to go heaven without accepting Christ is like a person who takes courses at the university but never registers. The courses do not count unless he registers with the front office. Those who register will graduate one day, but if you don't register, you can't graduate.

Dad may have had his own personal concept of religion, but he still respected Mom's faith, and he actually respected and feared Mom's faithfulness and Godly convictions. Dad knew that within that little old Black lady and that little kind heart was an awesome power. A power that exceeded earthly powers and could only come from love, and God is love. I later found out that the power Mama possessed came from the gift of the Holy Spirit in her life. I thank God that I had a praying Mama. She could get in touch with God in an instant. Her faith enabled her to have an instant connection with God and that saved my butt many times. I know it was because I had a praying Mama that I was able to get out of trouble situations. I believe her vicarious faith kept me afloat when I found myself in deep waters.

Dad was always joking and exhibiting a sense of humor and doing crazy things, but I could detect a deep sense of respect he had for Mama. Dad's relationship to God was one of real fear. He was a godly man in his own way, but I'm afraid it wasn't God's way. Like many people today you can't come to God on your terms. God doesn't bargain for your soul. It is written, "*Behold, all souls are mine; as the soul of the father, so also the soul of the son is mine: the soul that sinneth, it shall die. But if a man be just, and do that which is lawful and right...And hath not oppressed any, but hath restored to the debtor his pledge, hath spoiled none by violence, hath given his bread to the hungry, and hath covered the naked with a garment; He that hath not given forth upon usury, neither hath taken any increase, that hath withdrawn his hand from iniquity, hath executed true judgment between man and man, Hath walked in my statutes, and hath kept my judgments, to deal truly; he is just, he shall surely live, saith the Lord God*" (Ezekiel 18: 4-5, 7-9).

My father later decided that it was time for us to leave. Dad, Mom and the five younger children gathered our things together and moved to a place called Amado, Arizona. Amado was a desert without people. It was a place where we lived in total isolation of human life. We were deep in the desert and no one ever came to visit. It was like being on the Island of Patmos, where the Apostle John was exiled in the Book of Revelation. There were wild beasts who threatened to eat us day and night, and total isolation.

The living conditions were even more primitive than Continental. We lived where there were no outhouses. We had the woods as our own personal restroom. The people were prejudiced and the school still practiced segregation even though it was supposed to be integrated. We prayed for deliverance, and God heard our prayers—or should I say Mama's prayers.

My father had gotten a job and had an opportunity to buy some land and possibly build a house. We hoped that we would be able to grow up in this new community and live there for the rest of our lives. We packed our belongings and said goodbye to Amado and hello to Rillito, Arizona. True happiness was Amado, Arizona, in our rearview mirror.

Rillito was a place where little boys grew up with lifetime friends; where little girls never forgot their first kiss; and where adults became Godly individuals. It was said of Rillito that "it was holy ground and those that walked upon that ground were precious in the eyes of God."

Yes, we did it, we moved to Rillito, Arizona. Its inhabitants later referred to it as the "Toe," which was a reference to the last syllable in the name Rillito.

The boys and girls who grew up in this community were called "Toe Boys" and "Toe Girls." Rillito was initially nothing more than just land, a few cabins, few houses and many outhouses. It was a place where many Blacks, Mexicans and Native Americans congregated in a camp as families to work for the Man. Now when I say the Man don't get me wrong. He wasn't always White, and in Rillito and Marana, the Man who owned the cotton fields was Chinese. It was a melting pot of cultures, and the main source of employment was in the cotton fields or working on the farms. Many would pick, pull, chop and gin cotton. I mean, if there was anything to do with cotton we did it. Sometimes we chewed on it, and many times we wiped our behinds with it.

We lived in the camp until we were able to buy an acre of land and three cabins. We were still in the Toe, but we lived in three separate cabins that faced each other in the shape of a triangle on our own acre of land. The cabins each had a tin roof until we were able to replace the tin roof with wood planks. We had a wood heater that would glow when we put too much wood inside. It would turn red, and the stove pipes that came out through the roof would get so hot we would have to go on the roof and sprinkle water on the roof to keep it from catching on fire.

I had to chop wood for the cooking stove and the heating stove. Our beds were crowded, and I could look out through the holes in the roof and count the stars. The roof wasn't rainproof and every time it rained it leaked. When the dust blew, which seemed almost every day, the dust would come through the cracks in the walls. The floors were dirt floors and we would sprinkle water on the floor to harden the ground. We didn't have a refrigerator; it was called an icebox. You bought ice from the iceman and put about fifty pounds in the icebox which kept things cool, not cold. Most of the families got subsidy food from town because we were so poor, and we all had gardens and animals. I ate so much welfare meat, peanut butter and cheese that I got sick of it. My mother would always come up with different ways of preparing the commodity food we received. It was a relief to eat a rabbit or quail once in a while instead of commodity handouts.

When someone slaughtered a hog almost every family got a part of that hog. We shared produce from the gardens that each family grew, and it wasn't unusual for a kid to be sent from house to house borrowing flour, sugar, salt, lard or whatever was needed. You could borrow anything from anybody, except money. I still remember who got certain parts of the hog. I remember who got the feet, who got the tongue, and which parts I took to each family at their request. It was this attitude of giving and sharing that brought this community together as a family. There was a bond in that place that we won't find again until we get to heaven.

There were several Christian families in the Toe, but there was a certain Black man and his family. In fact, most of the people in the Toe were Christians or want-to-be Christians. Mr. Robinson cared for the people and did all within his power to provide opportunities for the people to work. He was considered a contractor for the cotton farmers. The adults called him Doc, but we called him Dad. Doc was a very wise person, but he was nearly blind. He told me later in life that he would memorize the eye charts in the license bureau by going down the day before he was supposed to take the exam. He had to do this in order to pass the test. We would go riding with him and his kids, and whatever Doc bought for one, he bought for all. He would never show favoritism towards any of us, including his own. Doc had a big family. I can't remember all the people in Doc's family, because some of them were beyond my age, but I grew up with several, and we grew closer daily and became the best of friends.

Dad's (Doc's) family was and has always been very special and very precious in my life. The ones who were dear to me were Paul, Cleo and Jerry. Cleo became my dearest friend and was my age; Paul was my buddy and was two years older; and then there was Jerry, and he was the youngest. My relationship with Jerry was rather incredulous. He was young and like a baby to us. But as time passed, one thing I realized about Jerry was that the boy was weird.

We had outhouses in the Toe with two seats. I mean you could take someone with you if you wanted, and you both could sit right next to each other and take care of business. You could sit side by side and share magazines and newspapers while you used the restroom. The smell was odiferous, but after a while you got used to it and the flies. You could sit there and have a conversation with your buddy.

When I went to the outhouse (restroom) I had great respect for athletes and had determined that I would not use a page out of the newspapers or magazine that had the face of a famous athlete on it to wipe my behind. Jerry, on the other hand, didn't even care. He would wipe his butt with anybody's face showing on the page. He was disrespectful of great men like Jesse Owens, Babe Ruth, Jackie Robinson and even Joe Lewis. Of course, it could have been because he was too young to read and didn't recognize the athletes.

We would go to the outhouse together, only because no one else would go with Jerry because he was so strange. Someone had to go with him so he wouldn't fall in. I was a bit concerned, because I didn't want him playing around in there and getting sick like I did. Every time we went to the outhouse Jerry would have to take off all his clothes. The person with him had to wait until he got completely undressed. This boy would take off his socks, T-shirts, underwear and cap. Little Jerry had a ceremonial ritual he would do every time he used an outhouse.

I would get so upset and tell him, "That's why nobody wanted to use the bathroom with you."

Then he would complain that nothing would happen unless he was comfortable.

I told him once, "Jerry, I am not going to sit here and wait for you to dress and undress every time you get ready to use the restroom. Every time we come to the bathroom we have to wait for you to go through this ritual. Man, this is ridiculous. You could at least stop at your shoes or leave your cap on. Why do you have to take everything off?"

"What's a ritual?" he asked.

"Never mind, never mind, I don't have time to explain."

"A man must be comfortable when he do-do," Jerry remarked.

"What man!" I shouted. "Boy, three years ago you weren't even a human being."

He would then give me the pity-party look, and I would have to apologize. I still say he was weird.

I remember when I first met Doc's family. First, I met Cleo and Jerry. Let me tell you, them boys is where Black got its color. I mean they were the epitome of Black, or shall I say they personified Black. They were also ugly, but so were all the other boys in the neighborhood. In fact, I have never seen a pretty boy in all my life. I believe when boys start looking pretty to other boys, watch out!

When we first moved to the Toe, I went over to Cleo's one morning, because I wanted to see these little ugly Black boys and maybe have some conversation. I saw them in the yard next to the water tank where most people in the neighborhood came to get their drinking water. I was only about eight years old. While I was sitting there talking to Cleo and watching Jerry play on the ground, I looked up, and there was this gigantic dog approaching me. This was the most unusual dog I had ever seen. He looked like he was half-wolf and half-horse, and he was walking up to me grinning and farting. I'm serious, this dog would sit there looking at you, grinning and passing gas. When I first saw him he came towards me with this grin on his face as if to say, *I'm looking at dinner and this fool don't even know it.*

I told Cleo, as I shook from sheer terror and was trying to hold back my urine, "You had better stop him right now! All I have to do is snap my fingers or give a whistle and within a few seconds my pet lion will come from around the corner of our cabin and this dog is in a world of trouble." I shouted, "Stop him, Cleo, or your dog is history!"

Cleo yelled, "Stop, Duke, don't go any farther!"

They were scared and really thought all I had to do was snap my fingers and some mysterious lion would appear and tear old Duke to pieces. Of course, they didn't realize I was actually lying. I didn't have any lion, but that dog scared me.

I told Cleo and Jerry, "If you guys don't get this dog far from me it won't be long before he becomes lion do-do."

So Cleo and Jerry ran and grabbed Duke and tied him to the water tank. Old Duke was looking real ugly, growling, grinning and passing gas. What a relief, for a while there I thought I would have to show them boys how fast I could run. Then to my surprise, they started begging, "Please don't call your lion."

I almost felt sorry for them as the tears ran down their little chocolate faces.

Then I said with relief, "Look, I don't really have my lion here with me. The lion isn't really at the house, but I do have a lion. I was forced to send him back to Africa before we left our other house. We didn't have enough food to feed the lion. If we would have brought him with us I would have had to feed him a lot of things, like elephants, deer and every once in a while little Black kids much like yourselves, because lions will eat anything."

Then Jerry told Cleo, "He ain't got no lion, Cleo," but Cleo was still cautious and told Jerry, "Just shut up."

Then they went to their house and called me from the side door to come inside. I walked inside and there was their older brother sitting there waiting for my arrival. He was a few years older, and the minute I saw him I knew my case was shot. I knew that as soon as they told him I said I had a lion, it was over. I knew he was going to laugh aloud and put me down. I was hoping they wouldn't say anything about what had happened outside, but they were like a bad refrigerator, they couldn't keep anything, and they spilled the whole story.

They told him about the lion and that I said I would feed them to him, and that Duke was going to be lion do-do. I thought, *Ah man, if I could only put them in a stove and melt them down to chocolate bars I could sell both of 'em for a nickel.*

Their brother Luke was lying on his bed, but he got up and started thinking about what was just said. I could see wisdom was flooding his mind as he contemplated what to say. I thought, *Oh my God, here it comes.* He winks at me with one eye as though to say, Go along with me on this one. He then glanced at Cleo and Jerry and began speaking.

"Well, if the boy say he got a lion, it is possible that he does have a lion. Now if the lion is in Africa that's going to work out even better. It will give y'all more time to become friends and it gives Duke a chance to live longer."

He then turned to me and said, "Now is that right?"

"That's right," I victoriously responded. "That's absolutely right."

It was then that I realized he was a friend. He was the kind of person that no matter what kind of problem or story the kids would tell him, knowing deep within himself that it was total fabrication, he would somehow work around it so there was no embarrassment to anybody. As time passed my love for him grew even more. He taught me to play baseball and not to fear the batter while catching a baseball behind the plate.

"Concentrate on the ball," he would say. "You will never even see the batter swing if you concentrate on the ball."

I did what he said and later became a pretty good catcher. My love for the family grew and would continue to grow for the rest of my life.

There were other people in the Toe. They were scarce to none, but they were there. All the boys in the Toe were my best friends. It just depends on who was mad at whom, and that determined your friend for the day. We had something that no other community had and that was unconditional love. We had parents who cared and most of them served God, at least on Sundays.

It is written: "*Greater love hath no man than this that a man lay down his life for his friends*" (John 15:13, KJV). I believe with all my heart, even to this day, there are some who would be willing to make such a sacrifice of love.

There was another family who had a son that was the terror of the Toe, and they called him Frank. We referred to him as "Odds" which was a mispronunciation of his last name. The boy truly was odd. Actually, the boy was the first Black daredevil I'd ever seen. He got that reputation because he would try anything once.

There was a wino in the Toe called Cadillac. Cadillac summed up Frank when he said, "He is a fool, crazy and probably a wino." Now we are talking about an eight-year-old kid. I figured like this, Frank was too young to be a wino, but I accepted the other things Cadillac said about him.

Cleo told me, "Whenever you are around Frank, be careful, because you can't trust him."

This boy was violence personified. If a dog bit Frank, eventually Frank would catch up with him and bite him back. Even the mosquitoes were afraid to bite Frank. Cleo warned me and said, "When you approach him, he is going to hit you for no reason. That's why everyone says he's crazy."

I knew I would inevitably have the opportunity to meet Frank, since we would live in the same community together for the next twenty years. When I met Frank he did exactly what Cleo had said. Sure enough, he came up to me and wanted to fight. Now it didn't take more than one punch when I caught him with a right cross, and he hit the ground. When the boy got up off the ground he was one of the best friends I ever had.

Frank looked like an overgrown midget. He never combed his hair, loved chewing bubble gum and walked like he was modeling a muscle shirt from Sears and Roebuck. Pound for pound I would say that Frank grew up to be a better athlete than many of us. As we grew older we outgrew Frank, and he was short and stocky and slurred his speech when he talked. I can truly say I have never known anyone who had a greater love for his friends than Frank. If he didn't kill you, he would love you to death.

After I hit him with a right cross one day, he got up and said, "Now listen, good buddy, ol' pal, don't tell anybody that you knocked me down.

You see, I like you! I like your attitude and I like your style."

As he walked away rubbing his jaw, I heard him say under his breath, "And your right hand ain't bad either."

We were a trio. Cleo, Frank and I, we were the best of friends.

The other family I had the privilege of meeting was Duck's family. Now the first person in that family I met was Duck. Duck was a couple of years older than me, and he had a younger brother named Lee, and this boy took more trips in his mind than Jackie Robinson did to first base. I think Lee was destined to grow up tripping. His mind was always in never-never land, and he was like the little dog in *The Wizard of Oz* name Toto, but he never got back to Kansas. I think Lee was destined to stay in the Land of Oz forever.

Duck was a good friend and he kinda introduced me to the real world. One day we were looking for bottles so we could sell them for the deposit, and as we were walking I saw a dollar. Just as I was about to pick it up, Duck pushed me out of the way and grabbed the dollar.

Again, we were getting ready to catch the bus to go to our school Christmas play, and Duck and I got into an argument. I wasn't paying much attention to Duck when he hit me in the mouth and started running. I chased him but to no avail.

Again, when we were in the line to get lunch one day, Duck got into an argument with a kid named Manny.

Manny told Duck, "I'm gonna kick your butt."

"Go for it," responded Duck. "Go ahead and take off your sweater and let's do it."

Manny made the mistake of attempting to take off his sweater so he could fight Duck. As he pulled the sweater over his head, I knew he had made the wrong move. Duck took advantage of this and started punching Manny, whose arms were stuck in his sweater. Poor Manny became a punching bag that day for Duck. After Duck had punched him several times, a teacher came over and stopped the fight. Manny finally got his sweater off, but it was too late, because the fight was over. Duck had kicked his butt.

We had this game that we played in the Toe. We made it up, and it was called Spondalay. Duck was one of the best at playing it. The rule was if you were eating anything or had something in your hand, you became a target for Spondalay. If a person said "Spondalay" and was fast enough to grab your food or knock the object out of your hand, he could keep what he grabbed. I believe Duck survived by playing that game.

As I grew older I gained respect for Duck and admired him because he showed me that friendship and loyalty were virtues endowed in him. I always saw him as someone trying to get over on you until this one day when my older brother Willie and my sister Kitty were involved in an argument. They were about to fight when my brother-in-law Herbert tried to stop the fight. Willie got mad and went and got a butcher knife and came back and stabbed Herbert in the chest during a scuffle.

Duck and I were watching this from the sidelines until the stabbing took place, and I went and tried to take the knife from Willie. We got in a wrestling match and though he was older and bigger than me, I was able to subdue him and take the knife, but not without injuries to my hand. Every finger on my right hand was sliced, because I grabbed the blade of the knife when I took it from Willie. Duck ran to Herbert and started ministering first aid to him the best he knew how. Being older, he had some idea of what to do. Blood was gushing from the open wound, and Duck helped him take off his shirt and held it over the wound.

We got him into a car and went with him to the hospital. The entire time Duck was holding the shirt over his wound and applying pressure. If he would not have done this, I believe my brother-in-law would have lost enough blood to go into shock, and he would have died. We did get him to the hospital in time and his life was spared. Herbert never told the police what happened to him, and by the time we got home, Willie had disappeared. I have never forgotten the loyalty and kindness Duck showed towards me and my family that day, but that was the type of love we shared in the Toe.

My cousin Gootee had followed us from Continental, Arizona, to Rillito. Gootee was my uncle's stepson. After living together for so long, he began to look and act like my uncle. Gootee was older than we were, but he was like an older crazy person. He was about three or four years older than my group, but he was the biggest prankster I have ever known. Sometimes I thought maybe he was "reality challenged."

Gootee gave most of the boys in the Toe nicknames. He gave Duck his name and said it was because he walked like a Duck. It seemed that Duck would walk a few feet then skip. He would then give off a sound like a hiccup. Gootee said he sounded like a duck.

My name was Colt, which later became Codas; Bernie's son Frankie was called Tater. Gootee said it was because he had a head like a potato. Since potatoes come in odd shapes, I could never figure it out until one day I took a good look Tater's head. He had all of his hair cut off and strange enough his head looked like a potato.

Gootee was no dummy; in fact, underneath the craziness was almost a genius. The boy was so crazy and extreme he very seldom woke up to the real world. There really is a thin line between genius and insanity, and Gootee was the only person in the world who could step back and forth across that line with great frequency. He was so capricious that whenever he showed up you never knew who you were talking to: the genius or the insane person; the balanced or the unbalanced.

There was a boy in the Toe who had a couple of nicknames. We called him DJ because he knew every song that came on the radio, or Hick because the boy was so country, he was bizarre. Now DJ was a twin and his twin sister was called Dank. Dank was a lot better looking than DJ, but she mostly stayed to herself. DJ was mysterious and weird. He was not like the other weird people in the Toe, but he was kinda smart weird. I believe DJ should have been an inventor. He had the most creative mind, but he could not practically bring his thoughts to reality. I think DJ lived well before his time. If Edison wouldn't have invented the lightbulb, DJ would have done it.

Then there was my friend Leroy who had the record for nicknames. We called him Jake, Dumpy, Dumb Dumpy, Fox and Jethro. Leroy was motion, athleticism, versatility, coordination, speed and sweetness all in one person. He was all these things personified. Now Leroy was the fastest thing on earth. He could run, catch, throw and shoot a basketball with both hands. He had problems trying to figure out which hand was dominant. He could swing a bat with either hand, but his left side was dominant. He shot a gun with his left hand, but he used his opposite eye for sighting. He shot a basketball with his right hand, ate with his left, threw a baseball with his right hand, and used either hand when he urinated. Leroy was ambidextrous, but we didn't know what to call it in those days so we said he was "even handed." The bottom line was that

Leroy had no idea of his potential or his greatness. O.J. Simpson, Walter Payton, Kareem or Chamberlin had nothing on Leroy. Leroy was great in athletics, but he didn't know it, and we certainly weren't going to tell him. The reason for this was because Leroy was no rocket scientist. In fact, the boy was kinda dumb. We figured if he didn't know he was exceptional, we certainly weren't going to bring it to his attention.

I remember walking from school one day with Leroy, and he looked up and saw the sun and the moon both in the sky. He was leaning against this telephone pole talking out loud, "Wow, man, how beautiful."

I asked him what he was talking about, and he says, "The earth, Codas, ain't it beautiful? I'm just 'zerving it."

I said to him, "What are you observing, Leroy?"

He replied, "Isn't it beautiful that I can stand here and see the earth and the sun at the same time?"

Now wasn't that dumb? He was looking at the moon and the sun and thinking he was looking at the earth and the sun.

I said to him, "Leroy, if that is the sun and the earth, then we must be standing on the moon. If not the moon, what planet do you think we are standing on?"

He got upset with me and said I was trying to confuse him, because the moon could never be seen in the daytime.

"You don't think I'm smart, but I am smarter than you all think, and I know that is the earth," Leroy replied adamantly.

So I agreed with him that he was indeed very smart, and if he wanted the moon to be the earth, why not?

Now, there were many other families in the Toe. Sylvester's family later on became a part of the Toe family. Syl (Sylvester) quite often got on my last nerve. Of course, there was his sister Lena, who Cleo and I saw as one of the guys as we were growing up.

I also had a friend who was three years older than us called Vetta, and she had a sister called Earley. V, as we often called her, was from a very talented family. The boys could really sing well and sang in the church. The girls, V and Earley, were very nice. V was very compassionate and Earley was very quiet. V was like a big sister, and I loved her in that respect. Both of them were very pretty girls, V being the oldest and Earley the youngest.

The other family who came to the Toe later was actually my relatives. They carried my mother's maiden name. The boys in this family were Sonny and his two younger brothers who never really came into the picture until they got older. Sonny had older sisters that were outside of our influence, except for Jessie, who was my age.

There was the Hunter family, and Morris was our age. He could never go anywhere or do anything. When his parents let him play with us, it was a miracle. But every now and then, he was allowed to be normal.

This about summed it up, except for a few others who will be mentioned later. We all were the families of the Toe. It seemed that all the kids belonged to all the parents and all the parents belonged to all the kids. We were a community of one big family, and the community raised the children.

The only problem with this was that you could never get away with anything. Any grownup had the right to spank or discipline any child and no one complained, not even the one being punished. If I did something wrong and Frank's mother punished me, when I got home I got it again from my mom. Mr. Tom, Duck's dad, would always say, "A hard head makes a soft butt."

The unity was one that you had never seen before, and was much different than today. Today, if someone whips your child, you either take them to court or shoot them on the spot. If they don't die, you can later have them arrested for child abuse.

CHAPTER FIVE

When Death Knocks

We hadn't been in the Toe very long when my brother Elbert got sick. He was older and had married a lady named Nancy. I knew that he drank a lot, and it affected him. One day when Elbert was resting, my sister Lou showed up and started meddling. She was causing so much hell, the devil was jealous of her. I think personally that Lou was a person who Satan was proud to have on his side. I do believe that there probably were times, though, that she did so well, he was jealous of her work attitude, and her integrity to always raise hell no matter where she went. I suppose that if the devil could have a sister, he would have chosen Lou.

Elbert got so frustrated with her that in order to shut her up, he started reaching for anything to throw at her. He grabbed an item and, with his eyes closed, he threw it at Lou as she was exiting the door with her tongue stuck out at him and his wife. Elbert never realized it was a knife (I don't think), but as it hit the door it stuck, just where Lou previously stood.

Lou ran home and told everyone that Elbert tried to kill her for no reason at all. She said she was just being nice and having a decent conversation when Elbert went berserk and threw a knife at her.

Elbert later got very sick and was taken to the hospital where he was diagnosed with a liver problem. I believe that he heard the Death Angel call his name, because as he waited for us to come and visit, he gathered all the gifts that had been given to him and distributed them to all the children. He gave away everything that was in his hospital room. I couldn't figure it out until the next day when we were told that he had passed away.

I wonder if he heard the voice of the Death Angel or was it the familiar voice of someone who had gone before him, like the voice of Bernice? We had his funeral, and it was sad, being so soon after the death of Bernice.

It wasn't long afterwards that Lou and I were walking from the store one night, and things got weird. Of course, with Lou things were always weird, but this time it was very different. I felt as if electricity was all over my body and my skin began to tighten. I wasn't afraid until Lou started screaming and running towards the house. I knew immediately that she must have felt the same thing. She ran, so I ran, straight to the door. We never bothered to turn the knob; we hit the door with a bang and poured in one on top of the other. Since I hit the door first, Lou was lying on top of me.

"What's wrong, what's wrong?" Mom and Dad shouted, as they saw us stacked on top of each other.

Lou was screaming, "Someone is chasing us! Someone is chasing us!"

I didn't have any idea why I was running. I just ran because Lou ran.

"Some man was just standing there watching us and then he started coming towards me," cried Lou as she peeled off me.

Dad went outside to look around and was gone for a few minutes. When he returned he had this look on his face as if he had seen a ghost.

He said, "It's all right, it was just Elbert. He was just playing around with Lou, but he didn't mean to scare Lace."

I have always wondered where Dad got that bit of information. Elbert had passed away a few months before. Did Dad really have a conversation with him, or was it intuition?

I believe as it is written, "*The living know that they shall die: but the dead know not anything, neither have they any more a reward, for the memory of them is forgotten*" (Ecclesiastes: 9:4, KJV). I don't believe in ghosts, but I do believe in spirits. I believe that spirit was evil, because its action served no good purpose.

One day at the Baptist church (we had two churches in the Toe: the Baptist and the Church of God in Christ), DJ's grandmother had a stroke and died. DJ and his twin Dank stayed with their grandmother, and she was the nicest person.

Someone once said, if you are a Christian, the place to die is in the church, but Mama said the best place to die is in Christ. I truly believed she died in Christ, because she was a beautiful person spiritually. She was also the one who kept their family together. She was a good cook, and I loved her pinto beans. I would go there for a breakfast of brother rabbit syrup with butter, some bacon or sausage and hot biscuits. She was the adhesiveness that held their family together. That was obvious, because after her death the family fell apart. Death had taken her from us, and when death knocks you must answer.

As I grew up, Cleo was considered my good friend, and Frank was my bad friend. It was like having good on one side and mischievousness on the other, but you love them both for their individualism. Let's be honest, Cleo didn't exactly wear a halo, and Frank didn't grow horns and carry a pitchfork, but they had two distinct personalities.

Frank, of course, was very mischievous, always into something and always fighting. Frank came by one day and wanted to go to the ditch (canal) where most of us went and cleaned up. We didn't have running water or electricity at that time and wouldn't get it for a few years, so the ditch played an important part in our lives.

Frank said he wanted to dig around the ditch bank because he was sure there was gold in the dirt. Now as intelligent as I am, I could not figure out why I let Frank talk Syl and me into this charade. I was not stupid, and Syl wasn't that dumb. We knew there wasn't any gold in the dirt, but I knew Frank was up to something. My curiosity kept me anticipating what was going to happen next. Frank was very confident and began singing a song.

"We're gonna find gold, we're gonna find gold…."

Then it happened, Frank began to pull dollar bills out of the dirt. I was thinking, *I can't believe this. It must be the song.*

Syl and I begin singing too. "We're gonna find gold," but we could not find anything.

Frank would sing for a while then he would say, "Hey, I found something."

We would go running over to Frank, and he would pull a dollar out of the ground. Now, of course, the money was only popping up where Frank was digging. I should have realized if that money had been buried for a period of time it shouldn't come out of the ground as crisp dollar bills. Frank dug around that dirt until he found ten dollars.

We eventually decided our digging time was over and spending time was now in effect. We had found enough money for three days of work. I thought to myself, *There is a time and season for all things, a time to dig, and a time to spend what you found while digging.*

We went to the store, and since Frank had all the money, we had to go along with his terms. He told us we are only going to spend a dollar and we would save the rest. You must understand that back then ten dollars was three days' wages.

We sent Frank in the store to buy something we could all share. We even gave him a grocery list and waited patiently for his return. You know back then things were really cheap, so when he came out with this big bag, we knew we were going to chow down. He then poured out onto the ground one hundred bubble gums. Of course, they cost a penny each.

Syl and I were furious.

We told Frank, "Man, we're hungry from all that digging and we sent you in to buy food, not this mess. We were thinking Hostess Twinkies, MoonPies, bologna ends, summer sausage, Hires root beer, R.C. colas, Delaware Punch, and you come out here with one hundred bubble gums! Nigga, are you crazy?"

"Don't panic," he said, "this is just the beginning."

Now, since Frank had found the gold in the first place, we really couldn't complain, especially when he decided to split it with us. We divided three into one hundred, and it came out that I got ten, Syl got ten and Frank got eighty. That's what happened when you use "Frank division" instead of long division. Perhaps, flunking math may have had something to do with his poor division skills, or just maybe, he was smarter than we thought.

We all had a mouthful of bubble gum and were happily chewing and blowing bubbles when Frank's older brother Mutt jumped out from behind the bushes. He threw us on the ground and told us that he was going to kill both of us, because we had stolen ten dollars out of his wallet. It then dawned on me that this Negro (Frank) done stole that boy's money and was about to get us killed. Syl and I were on the ground looking up at Mutt, terrified, not able to talk with all this bubble gum in our mouth.

Mutt was swearing and shouting, "Who stole my money! Who stole my money?"

We couldn't talk with his hands around our necks and a mouthful of bubble gum. Mutt was too angry to realize that unless he released pressure from around our necks, no sound could come out. Now the irony of this was that Frank escaped, and we were with this mad man who was trying to exterminate us. He seemed to be hoping that the gum in our mouth would turn back to money. Mutt told us that he knew that Syl and I took the money, because Frank wouldn't do such a thing.

Syl found enough breath to say, "Nigga, please!"

I wondered how he could think of Frank as being so innocent. That boy could steal the sweetness out of sugar.

We were pleading for our lives when Frank yelled out to Mutt, "Hey, fool, I stole your money and bought me one hundred bubble gums, so turn them boys loose, now!"

Mutt's countenance was distorted with rage and had the look of mass destruction on it. If you could have looked into his eyes, you could have seen in his pupils the reflection of two little caskets with Frank in them both. He got off of us and dusted himself off, and without even an apology he started running after Frank. I knew that Frank was a dead child, and I would never see him again. Of course, at that moment we didn't really care, and we were hoping that Mutt would catch up with him. I didn't want Mutt to kill Frank, just to dangle his unconscious severely battered body in the doorway of death for a moment. But Frank did something very smart. As he ran, every so often he would drop a dollar. Mutt, of course, would have to stop and pick up the dollar. Mutt stopped nine times which allowed Frank to escape and us as well. Frank was our hero even though he almost got us killed; he turned right around and saved our lives.

Mutt was married to my cousin Zelma, and the one thing that has always stood out in my mind was that she was indeed the most beautiful woman I have ever seen. She had caramel skin with a smile that could light up a room. I have never seen anyone with such natural beauty. She could have been a poster girl for a beauty magazine. Even as a child I noticed how she turned heads as she passed by lustful eyes. Little did I know that the Death Angel was preparing to visit her.

When you are a growing boy in the Toe, and your parents leave a certain amount of food with you to eat while they are working, it will always run out. Everyone knows that a child can't ration food. You normally ate all the meals at once and spent the rest of the day repenting and hungry. Sometimes I would be very hungry and there was nothing at home to eat until our parents got home from work. I would pray and God would answer my prayers.

I would hear a voice tell me to go to the store, and I would find money on the way to buy what I needed. Each time I did this I would find enough money to buy a candy bar or a bologna end at the store. I had so much faith that I would tell my sister Lou I was going to the store to get some food. I wasn't familiar with the scripture that said, "*... Ye have not, because ye ask not*" (James 4:2, KJV), but I exercised my right to ask many times.

Lou, being a skeptic, would say, "You ain't got no money, fool."

But I would go and always return with something to eat. Once, I felt the sensation to go to the store because there would be money there for me. I told Lou and again she reminded me that I was broke and Black, and I would be that way when I returned.

"Fool, you gonna leave here hungry and you gonna return here hungry!" she shouted as I walked out.

I went anyway, and by the time I got there I still hadn't found anything. It was raining so hard that I got in the phone booth for protection. I accidentally clicked the return change handle and out came fifty cents worth of change. I went inside and bought some goodies to eat and when I returned home I told Lou about it. She crossed her fingers in front of her face attempting to make a cross like on the vampire movies and said, "Get back, demon brother, get back!"

She then threatened to put a stake through my heart when I went to sleep. She went to the kitchen cabinet and found some garlic salt and threw it in my direction. I was about to leave when I decided to share my blessing with her. I showed her the fruits of my prayer, and though she said I was possessed, she still ate the food.

CHAPTER SIX

The Do-Do Bug

The Toe was a jamming place. I mean, on Friday and Saturday nights we partied hard while the older folk tried to kill each other. On Sunday morning we all went to church and thanked God for those who made it through Friday and Saturday night.

One night we were all "partying down" and the old folk hadn't started shooting at each other yet. My cousins had built additions to their houses, and they had added on a gambling room and a café for people to eat and dance.

One night Leroy had ticked off his older brother Lewis to a high degree of pisstivity. Lewis decided that night Leroy would die. Of course, Lewis tried to kill somebody every weekend after he got drunk. The only problem with this was that I was often mistaken for Leroy. So while we are dancing to Otis Redding, Fats Domino, BB King and Lightning Hopkins, we got the news that Lewis was going to kill Leroy, and he was heading in our direction.

Lewis was the type of person that didn't remember anything you did to him until he got drunk, then he remembered everything from the day he ever met you. Frank and I told Leroy to get away from us, because if Lewis didn't kill him, we would.

Sure enough, someone started yelling, "Lewis is coming with a gun!"

We all started running for our lives, and Frank and I were together as we ran. We hid behind a cabin that was nearby and were leaning against it, tired and breathing hard with our backs against the cabin. Frank whispered that he heard Lewis say he was going to kill every male child, then later check the faces of the bodies to see if Leroy was among them. Now, since I was often mistaken for Leroy, this was not good news.

Frank and I were terrified as we inched our way around the cabin in the dark shadows of the night. It was so dark that we bumped into someone also hiding and to our surprise it was Leroy. This boy was determined to get us killed. The thought flashed across our minds, perhaps we could render him unconscious and give him to Lewis as a peace offering. At that moment we heard Lewis coming, so we threw Leroy out in front of Lewis. We hoped that Leroy, being the friend that he was, wouldn't mind sacrificing himself for his friends. We realized the sacrifice he was about to make, but if anyone could escape, we knew Leroy could do it.

Leroy lived about fifty yards away from where we were hiding, but when Leroy left that spot his feet hit the ground maybe twice before he was opening the door. Man, I realized at that moment, the boy was gifted. Lewis was so drunk he never saw Leroy. If he had seen Leroy he wouldn't dare go to his mother's house. Mrs. Tiny (their mother) was probably the only person who wasn't afraid of Lewis. She would have taken that gun and put it up Lewis's anatomy, and would have caused his bowels to be blocked for a week.

Finally, the grownups caught up with Lewis, tied him up and took him home until he got sober, which was the next day. They untied him, of course, before he woke up, knowing that if they didn't, the next weekend they would be on Lewis's hit list. Of course, with Lewis, everything that happened to him while he was drunk would seem to be a dream. He thought the guys were just a dream, and his trying to kill us all was only a figment of his imagination. The next weekend when he got drunk again his memory would return, and everyone was in trouble.

One night my cousin and a neighbor called D.C. were having a shootout. It was like watching a battle from the Civil War right there in front of you.

D.C. was shooting at Cousin Sammy from behind his car and Cuz was hiding behind his car shooting at D.C. I fried some potatoes and got some Kool-Aid in a jar and sat on a stump and watched the show from our backyard. They never hit each other; in fact, I never saw the bullets hit anything, but it was exciting. D.C. had his kids reloading his gun, but Cuz reloaded his own. I knew if they made it through the shootout they would be in church the next day.

The next morning all of those who survived Saturday night went to church. I remember the sermon that morning was about the rooster and the peacock. The pastor told a story about a rooster who ruled over all the chickens in the pen. This was his Easter sermon about how we are so often deceived and blame others for things they had nothing to do with. I wondered if this was because of the fight between D.C. and Cuz.

He told the story about a rooster that was in love with this hen that was sitting on a bunch of eggs ready for hatching. There was a peacock that the rooster never liked and oftentimes suspected him of playing around with the hens. He seemed jealous of the peacock. One day, when the hen got off the eggs for a while, some of the kids painted the eggs different colors. When the rooster saw the different-colored eggs, naturally he became suspicious of the peacock. When the eggs hatched, something weird happened. All the chickens appeared to be of different colors. The pastor said the rooster, seeing this, became very upset. He went to the back of the chicken coop and damn near killed the peacock.

That was when I realized that things were not always what they seemed. Maybe this was meant for the ones involved in the shooting, but neither of them was in attendance.

This reminded me of my sister Lou. Lou must have been conceived out of anger. We tried to convince her many times that she wasn't a part of the family and that we had found her near a cactus plant. Now Lillie, we called Lou, was the biggest liar in the entire universe and was all the time perpetrating defecation among everyone. We had come to the conclusion that if everyone in the community of Rillito were given the privilege to kill their worst enemy, only one person would have died. I believe everyone would have picked Lou. This girl was bad personified, and her name should have been "She-Bad."

She lied, stole, assaulted people, beared false witness against them, gambled, tried to smoke cigarettes, drank hard liquor and cheated: those were just the charges brought against her by the family.

When she wanted to be spiteful, she would wear Daddy's underwear, steal food out of the refrigerator, cook food that wasn't edible, and tried to kill the family several times with meals she prepared. She was the only girl I knew who would pass gas deliberately and curse like a sailor.

One time I came to the house with a friend name Lee. This was the boy who took trips without leaving the Toe. All his trips took place in his mind. That day Lou started her normal name-calling and making accusations. She started cursing our whole family and going completely through the genealogy. Lou talked about family members I didn't know we had. She didn't care if they were living or dead, and she had something to say about everyone.

I had had enough and my pisstivity level had reached the state of volatile. I grabbed her and began to choke her as she was trying to spit on me with that acid spit of hers. Now, you know that this girl didn't brush her teeth, so if she would have spit on me, my arm probably would have melted off. While I'm choking big Lou, Lee was trying to pull me off of her, but I am thinking in my mind, *The only way to get rid of this is to kill it!* I tried to put my fist in her mouth, but I couldn't and to this very day she has a gap between her two front teeth where I tried to divide them. I couldn't pull her hair, because Lou's natural needed Miracle-Gro just to reach the surface. Trying to grab Lou's hair would be like trying to catch a mosquito by his eyelids.

Lee finally pulled me off while pleading for mercy for Lou. I stopped choking her to please Lee, and as I got up and begin walking out the door, I felt this pain on my back. As I turned I discovered Lou had planted a broom between my shoulder blades. I turned and grabbed her neck again and was firing on her with my left hand, and she tripped and fell down. So I straddled her, and I was trying very hard to separate her head from her shoulders, but her head wouldn't come off.

Finally, Lee pulled me off of Lou again, and then Lou died. Let me explain to you that Lou really didn't die. One thing for sure is that Hollywood doesn't have any stuntmen who could perform as well as Lou when it came to dying. This was not the first time Lou died; in fact, every time Lou got into a fight and was losing, she would die. If you said something to Lou that made her angry or hurt her feelings, she would just die. Heart attacks and strokes were her favorite method of dying. The strokes consisted of her having paralysis in certain parts of her body and then having convulsions before she died, and it took some time before she died. She carried this out to the fullest. She would stiffen her body and drool at the mouth, then fall over dead. It was a very convincing acting job on how to die.

One day she put some baking powder in her mouth and foam came out as if she was rabid. I thought this was a very creative on Lou's part. She would feign convulsions, and she was able to have muscle spasms only on one side of her body to make it look real. Sometimes the family would applaud her death scene, because she was the best. The heart attacks were often quick, but very dramatic. They didn't normally drag out like the strokes. Her eyes grew big, and she would grab her heart, most of the times on the left side, but when she forgot which side her heart was on she would grab the right side. We would remind her during the death scene and she would correct herself. She would then start trembling and her whole body would tighten up. When she died she would relax her body and exhale completely. All the air would leave her body, and she would grow limp. This was professional acting if I'd ever I seen it.

Sometimes we would be at the eating table, and we would say something about her little biddy natural, request that she use water next time she bathed or give her an invitation to leave the family, and immediately she would die. I mean she would drop her whole face right into the potato salad or corn bread, it didn't matter, and Lou had a big face. She would roll her eyes back into her head, slobber, start shaking and pretend to be paralyzed, grab her chest and die right there at the table. Man, you don't die and let your face fall in the food. We had to eat that food after she died in it, but it didn't seem to matter to Lou.

Meanwhile, she had completely fooled Lee, and he thought she was dead. I knew better, because I had killed Lou many times in the past, and whenever I came back home she was always alive again. Poor Lee, he was kneeling next to Lou, giving her last rites and telling me that I had killed my sister. I grabbed Lee and drug him out of the house and slapped him a couple of times to bring him back from his trip, because he was really starting to believe that I had actually murdered Lou. We walked to the store and I told him that I had killed Lou many times, but she would be alive and well when we returned.

Lee and I went to the store and bought some candy and returned to the house. When Lee opened the door and saw Lou still lying on the floor, he started thinking that Lou was sure enough dead. There she was, still lying on the ground pretending. This threw Lee off the deep end. Lee went back to tripping and thinking that he was an accessory to the crime. He was contemplating aloud on how we could get rid of the body and what we should say to the detectives.

Well, as I'm looking at Lou, I noticed something strange. This wasn't the way she was lying when we left. I noticed the girl had grease stains on her lips, face and eyebrows. I went to the kitchen, and sure enough, there was the evidence. This girl done got up, fried her some potatoes, onions and bacon and had eaten. When she saw us coming back she lay down on the ground, totally switched around from her original position, and was pretending to be dead.

Lee was now kneeling beside Lou, praying and asking God to forgive us and bring this devil back to life. Lou was trying very hard to keep from laughing, but Lee had stolen the show with his plea for divine mercy and intervention. Now, Lou couldn't hold it any longer, and she exploded with laughter, literally scaring the hell out of Lee. He was thinking she had gone over to the other side, so when she burst out laughing in his face, it was too much to handle. The boy screamed like a girl and fainted right there in front of me. I don't know if he wasted soda on the front of his pants or if that was urine, but his pants were wet.

Lou was laughing out of control and saying that she knew we were both fooled, and our hearts had stopped from fear when we thought she was dead. I let her know, as I proceeded to wake Lee from his faint, that I wasn't taken in by her antics.

Lee woke up and jumped up screaming like a girl and yelling, "The dead has risen, the dead has risen!"

He ran out of the house and didn't stop until he got home. I don't know what he told the rest of his family, but all the doors and windows started slamming shut.

Sunday morning Mama wasn't feeling well, so she sent her offering to the church by Lou. While the preacher was up talking, ol' crazy Lou walked in and went to the front of the church. Now, the pastor was known for his quick-wittedness. He stopped talking, and he along with the rest of the congregation watched Lou as she approached the offering table in front of the pulpit.

After interrupting him and saying aloud, "Here, Mama sent her offering!" Lou threw the money on the table and walked away in her fashionable manner, shaking what behind she had and holding her head up in arrogance. I'm glad she didn't take a bow because half the time Lou didn't wear any underwear. The pastor looked at the money on the table and stared at Lou, then commented, "Well, I know the Lord sent the offering, but the devil brought it."

It wasn't long afterwards that Lou had ticked off everybody in the Toe. I mean the girl had sown discourse throughout the community and created a dissonance among all the occupants. The entire community was ready to revolt against each other, and there was only one avenue of releasing this anger and wrath. I told everyone that if we killed Lou the problem would go away, but since I was so young they wouldn't listen. I know they wanted to kill Lou, but they couldn't figure out how to do it and not be arrested. I figured if everyone in the community wanted her eliminated that would be a good defense in court. If we wounded her enough to get her to court and let the judge see the type of person she was, he would probably let us finish her off.

The Toe was ready for a civil war. This was the first time a single person would be responsible for a civil war. If such a thing was possible, only Lou could do it. I mean, the adults rebelled against their children. The children all wanted to leave, the domestic animals no longer wanted to cooperate, and the wild animals in the desert were threatening to move into the city.

I suggested we should hide her in a cave for fifty years and not feed her. If we did that we could get rid of her and at the same time keep her from multiplying, but again they thought I was too young to make a suggestion and no one would listen.

Now we had to prepare to fight a civil war in the town of Rillito. We had in the southern portion of the Toe a huge cottonwood tree that was for romance. There were also two great big walnut trees for fighting or ironing out disputes. These trees are where we had picnics on the nineteenth of June and where we celebrated birthdays of prominent individuals. They provided walnuts, of course, for us to eat and the walnut trees provided a battleground for us to fight the civil wars. That was where many disputes were settled, and a child or two conceived.

All the children had left the Toe and were headed for the walnut trees along with the animals. The roaches, of course, stayed home and were grateful for everything that Lou had done, knowing this was their opportunity to come out and have a feast. Of course, there were a few domesticated animals that followed us to the walnut trees, hoping to see her demise.

We all went down to the walnut trees with Lou leading us. We decided that when we got there all the families were going to fight. Lou had all the families against each other due to her lies. Since Lou's latest victim was my cousin Gootee, we all decided to let Lou and Gootee fight first. Everybody knew that Lou was the cause of all the dissonance and conflict. We also knew she couldn't fight and the first time someone hit her or started to win the fight she was going to die right there on the spot. We decided that if Lou died in the first fight, the war would be over and the revolution would not have to be fought. We all knew Lou was the perpetrator of all the evil and tumult.

Now, Gootee was crazy, but everyone was curious as to whether there would really be a fight, because we knew that Gootee would never hit a girl. Of course, Lou wasn't a girl, she was my sister, "the horror of the Toe."

There was a contract put out on Lou and many folk were trying to get her terminated. Someone had mentioned that the price on Lou's head was "five dollars dead and nothing if she lived." I don't know who put the money up, but I was told they would throw in fifty bubble gums.

Big Lou was under the walnut trees and standing near the canal, meddling, sticking her tongue out at Gootee and trying intensely to provoke him. She was also trying very hard to sneak up to him to throw a punch. Lou finally got close enough and took a swing at Gootee. We all knew that Gootee was fast and quick and couldn't be hit. He stepped out of the way of Lou's punch with ease. We were not surprised of his speed, because according to Huey (Gootee's cousin), Gootee was the only person in the Toe who was faster than the "do-do bug."

Now, if I can interrupt for a moment and explain this to you, the story goes like this: There was a do-do bug in the Toe, but no one had ever seen this bug. He was so fast that all you ever saw was the remains he left behind. Huey gave Gootee this title, because earlier in our lives, like about two months prior, allegedly Gootee was supposed to have caught a do-do bug. I was there when Huey gave Gootee the title of being faster than the do-do bug.

I knew the true story and Gootee never caught a do-do bug. I remember when the situation actually happened. We were down by the railroad tracks looking for signal lights (flares) when Gootee, being mischievous, decided he was going to play a trick on Huey. We all knew Gootee was a trickster, and why Huey could never figure it out, I do not know. Huey was no dummy and was the only person I knew who got straight A's in all his special education classes.

I saw Gootee go behind the bushes and put his homemade paper bag hat over some dog do-do. Huey came along and observed Gootee holding the hat down as if he had caught something under it. He asked Gootee what was under the hat, and of course, Gootee told him he had caught the fastest bug in the world: the do-do bug.

Gootee began his little scheme by telling Huey, "I heard you were next to me in speed and quickness so I would like you to prove it. I'm gonna give you a dollar if you can catch this bug before he leaves from under this hat."

Huey got down on his knees, put his chin on the hat, stretched out his arms around the paper hat and gave Gootee the signal to move it.

Gootee was laughing and about to lose control, but held the hat steady and told Huey to close his eyes. Huey closed his eyes and grabbed for the bug as Gootee lifted the hat. The boy ended up with a handful of dog do-do. Even his little biddy natural had do-do in it. Gootee was laughing so hard when Huey looked up at him with the look of sorrow and failure, knowing that he done missed the fastest bug in the world. Gootee told Huey, "I told you! I told you this was the fastest bug in the world. Boy, the bug done do-doed and gone!" That day Huey gave Gootee the reputation as being "faster than the do-do bug."

Now back to the fight: Lou's punch missed Gootee and he reached out and made the stupid mistake of trying to grab Lou's hair. You can't grab Lou's hair, because it only reached one-quarter inch in the peak of growing season. He couldn't grab her hair so he accidentally slapped her nappy head as he reached out. Lou fell backwards into the canal and did a beautiful backflop, landing in the water. She didn't have on any panties and exposed her butt to all the civil war participants as she fell into the water.

I was watching Lou flop around in the water and everyone thought she was only pretending to drown so no one tried to help her. I knew everyone was thinking that if she died the revolution was over. I thought, *She can't really swim so I'd better help her; after all, she is my sister.* While I'm contemplating whether I should save her or not, she climbed out of the water, staggered over to Gootee and threw herself on the ground near his feet. She stuck out her tongue and convulsed right there in front of us. She took a deep breath then exhaled and died beautifully. It was so touching and well done that many of the onlookers applauded. Frankly, I wanted to tie a boulder to her feet and throw her back in the water.

Everyone started cheering and saying, "The revolution is over! The revolution is over!"

We all left Lou down by the walnut trees dead, and decided to go farther down stream. Now since the revolution was over we all decided to go swimming. I knew that Lou would later get up and be at home when we got there, so I went swimming. Later on, I saw Lou going through the cotton field trying to get home without anyone seeing her. I don't know why, but I had a sense of relief knowing she was okay.

CHAPTER SEVEN

Exploits

We all started growing up, but Gootee was still playing jokes on people. I guess that part of him never grew up.

We decided to go swimming one day and Gootee played a trick on V. He found a stick and put some you-know-what on it and threw it in the water. Now, I don't know why Gootee would do this to any of the girls in the Toe, because they were all clean, except Lou. I mean, they were always polite and would never pass gas or spit in public, except for Lou.

While we were swimming in the canal, Gootee started yelling, "V, please help me, my house key is on that stick, please grab it for me!"

V grabbed the stick, being the compassionate person that she was, desperately trying to help. She grabbed the stick and the feces squished through her fingers. After looking at her hand and seeing her fingers stuck together, reality hit her like a ton of bricks, and she fainted in the water. We all jumped in the water to rescue V from her horrific ordeal, except Gootee, who ran away across the cotton field laughing.

There is no doubt in my mind that boy was a pervert. Huey called him a "prevert," but prevert or pervert, it described Gootee. Huey said a prevert was a pervert in the making.

We were in junior high school and Gootee was in high school. One day, while swimming down by the waterfall, Gootee went to stand above us on the bridge. At certain places along the canal there were floodgates.

When the floodgates were up, the water flowed under the gate and continued in the canal. If the gate was down, the water had to flow over the gates and it formed a waterfall on one side. While standing on the bridge, Gootee yelled down to Huey to get behind the waterfall and see if he could hear him count to ten. After the number ten, Huey was to come out and let him know if he could hear Gootee counting. Gootee would count to eight and stop.

When Huey came out from under the waterfall he would tell Gootee, "I can't hear you past the count of eight."

So Gootee told him, "Let's try it again."

Gootee started to count, but this time he took out his "thing" (penis) and started to pee where he thought Huey was going to come up out of the water. He started counting up to ten, and when Huey came out, he looked upward, thinking the water was still hitting him in the face. Poor Huey didn't realize crazy Gootee was peeing on his head. Like always, Gootee ran home before Huey realized what had happened. Of course, we did enlighten him.

The next day Huey and I decided to meet at the canal to go swimming and to take a bath, without the presence of Gootee. This was an everyday event, especially since there were no showers in the Toe. I dreaded walking by Leroy's house, because I knew he would stop me. I walked by Leroy's anyway, and sure enough, he was out by the chicken coop, and he spotted me. I was wearing my swimming trunks and I had a towel in one hand, soap in the other hand. I didn't have on a shirt, but I was wearing rubber thongs on my feet.

Leroy, seeing all this, yelled, "Hey, Codas, come here. I have something to ask you."

He beckoned for me to come to him and I really didn't want to go, because I knew what he was going to ask. All of those clues just didn't register with Leroy. Sure enough, as I walked up to him, he asked the question, "Hey, Codas, where you going?"

I retorted, "Leroy, take a good look at me. I have on swimming trunks, no shirt, pair rubber sandals on my feet; towel and soap in my hand and an Afro fork stuck in my hair. Where do you think I'm going?"

He scratched his head for a second then answered, "I think you're going swimming. It's hard to tell, because there are hardly any clues."

I was finally able to get away from Leroy after a brief conversation and meet Huey at the canal. While Huey and I were in the canal swimming, Leroy showed up and wanted to swim with us. That boy could do anything in the world but swim well. Huey, myself, Frank and Lee, who had later joined us, decided to lure him away from the ditch. Leroy could do some things that just weren't natural. This boy was one of the first to run on water in the Toe.

We had a gate that could be raised or lowered like a shutoff valve and the water would spring out from under the gate when you lowered it just enough. When it was lowered the water on one side got deeper and the water on the other side became shallow and swift as it squirted forward. Leroy could actually run on the water going upstream and grab the gate when he reached it. The rest of us would get caught in the current and swept downstream. Very seldom were any of us able to imitate Leroy. We were kind of jealous that he could do this with such ease. So, to avoid the running on the water phenomenon, we went to the big cottonwood tree and started climbing it. This got Leroy's attention and he joined us.

Leroy began to climb the tree and climbed almost to the top. This tree was over eighty feet high. While Leroy was climbing, Frank found some matches and was burning some weeds under the tree. When Leroy saw the fire he was drawn to it like a magnet. He climbed downward and ended up right above the fire. We encouraged him to jump from where he was. We told Leroy to jump over the fire, but everyone knew that fire was a magnet, and of course, it drew his foot right to it. Leroy landed in the fire and the weeds stuck to his foot, and his foot was on fire. After about a minute of some serious hopping up and down, we put the fire out and convinced Leroy that we had saved his life. We didn't want him to go home and tell his mama that we tried to kill him. He was the youngest boy in his family and his parents treated him like precious ointment.

We then went over to the canal at a point where the water was very low. Some days the water level was high enough that we could actually dive in from off the side of the ditch bank. I was walking slowly with Leroy because of his burnt foot, and when we got to the canal, the guys were all swimming around. Frank and Lee were kneeling in the water pretending to be standing, but Huey was actually standing next to them, and you can see the water level was low because there was no way that Huey was three feet taller than the others. I saw this, and I'm thinking Leroy must see this also.

Frank and Lee were yelling at Leroy, telling him, "Dive in, Fox, the water level is high today."

They kept telling Leroy, "Go ahead, Dumpy, dive in, you can do it."

Leroy responded, "I'm not going to dive into that shallow water. I could hurt myself. I know the water is lower than what you say."

Now, about that time Huey got the message from the other two and was sitting in the water.

They're shouting to Leroy, "The water has risen! Come on in, the water has risen!"

Before I could tell him that it was a trick, the fool dove into three feet of water headfirst and hit his head on the bottom of the canal. When he came up out of the water, we realized that the bottom was harder than Leroy's head. We were all terrified because blood was running down his face. Leroy started crying and hopped home on one foot holding his head. It was a sight to see as he hopped all the way home.

He told his mother that we tried to cremate his foot and tried to kill him in the ditch. I don't think the word cremate was in Leroy's vocabulary, but that was the word used when his mama came down and whooped us all. She sent us all home and our mamas whooped us again. We all loved ol' Leroy, but that day loving him was hard. It's hard to love someone with your heart when your butt is on fire because of them.

We were very creative in those days, and we had some homemade bows and arrows, and we had this little gang we called the Nightriders. It was nothing like the gangs today that go around killing children, but a more wholesome type. That night we knew it was time for the Nightriders to ride. We were like Robin Hood and his Merry Men. We took from the not so rich and gave it to the very poor. We would go hunting and kill rabbits, and we would steal watermelons and cantaloupes from the Man, and would leave them at the doorsteps of the Toe families.

The White man and the Chinaman knew it was a lot of little Black Zorros and Robin Hoods who came to steal their watermelons and that's why he would pack rock salt in his shotgun shells. I think he really enjoyed shooting at us, and since no one got hurt, we didn't really care. There were many nights, though, my booty burned because of the impact of rock salt. It was like a trade-off: a hot booty for a cold melon.

That night Paul and Duck were with us. Huey got stuck in between a barbwire fence while carrying two stolen melons. I was lying down on my stomach and Carl (another friend) had two watermelons under his arms, and he was running through the field, which was also occupied by some horses. It was pitch black and you could barely see objects a few feet away. The upset horses got the Man's attention and when he put the light on Carl it gave Huey and I time to get away. Carl made it to the Blue Lizard (our car), and Huey and I were still crawling through the field when we come across two horses lying down. I thought that was odd, because you never see horses lying down, then I realized both of them had been knocked unconscious and were staggering and trying to stand up.

We finally made it to the Blue Lizard and the Gray Stallion (Paul's truck) and everyone was safe. Carl told us that he had run into something. He fell to his knees, but didn't turn loose his melons. That's when I figured out that Carl, that Negro, had run into the two horses and knocked them out.

We all gathered up what few melons we had and started to leave. It was then we realized that DJ was missing. I thought to myself, *Oh my God! What if he got shot and was seriously injured?* My heart began to pound, but I wouldn't reveal my feelings to the others.

"Let's go look for DJ," responded those who had made it to the vehicles safely.

We drove around the melon patch with our lights out, hoping to run into DJ, and we literally did just that. I saw this figure come out of the melon field and crash into my right front fender.

Everyone begin screaming, "It's DJ! It's DJ! He's alive!"

Apparently DJ had stolen a wheelbarrow from the Man and had been loading watermelons and hiding them close to the road. The boy had forty-one watermelons. We had watermelons sitting in our laps and all around us. That night the Nightriders were able to leave watermelons at the front door of every family in Rillito.

The next day I heard my mother saying, "Those Nightriders done did it again, and they left watermelons at everybody's doorstep."

Our parents told us, "You boys need to be like them Nightriders, they do good things and help the people, but y'all just play all day and eat up everything in house."

We just kept playing as if we didn't hear them. If only they knew.

The next time we went out we were hunting rabbits and sidewinder rattlesnakes. Our parents would allow us to drive if we were going hunting or to the garbage dump. We ate the rabbits, but the snakes were a different kind of a challenge. We would find sidewinder rattlesnakes in the desert and make them mad enough to chase us. Don't let anyone tell you that an angry snake won't chase you.

After being out most of the night, we decided it was time to go home, because the car was almost out of gas. We found some combines in the fields and ciphered gas out into the Blue Lizard until it was full. Being tired and sleepy, we decided it was time to go home, but Frank, whose turn it was to drive, decided he wanted to drive around in the fields to see what else he could steal. At this point in our lives we were only about twelve or thirteen years old.

Frank fell asleep and ran into a river. Now, I'm not talking about a stream of water, I mean this boy ran into the Santa Cruz River. Of course, the Santa Cruz very seldom had water in it unless it rained. This night was an exception, and it peaked at about three feet. When we woke up we could see water all around us. Lee woke up and started doing overhand strokes like he was swimming. He was hitting everybody in the face and screamed like a sissy, "I'm drowning, I'm drowning!"

We all yelled, "Fool, shut up, you're in the car and the windows are up!"

We climbed out of the car safely, one by one, cussing Frank every inch of the way. We were really angry with Frank, because he had the nerve to tell us, "Well, y'all had gone to sleep, so I had the right to sleep too."

I had to explain to him in an articulate manner that he didn't have that privilege if he was driving. "Fool, you're driving, you can't sleep because if you sleep you will probably drive into a river or something."

Frank replied, "Not necessarily!"

We sent a couple of guys to Richard's house. Richard was one of the White kids who was color-blind. He was the quarterback and a good friend. His family was always sympathetic toward the Toe Boys and encouraged us in every way possible. His father had a little farm and a tractor, so we borrowed it.

I don't know how we managed, but that night we got home and

everyone slept in the car in front of my house. Feet were stuck out the window of the car. Some were asleep on the top of the car and on the fender, and DJ was freaking everybody out because the boy slept with his eyes open. It's hard to know if the boy was awake, asleep or dead.

Later, we decided we needed a more "serious weapon" for the future. We were tired of chasing rabbits and birds with homemade bows and arrows and slingshots. I thought about it and I came up with the answer. My dad had a shotgun named "Ol' Betsy" and he said he would let me use it one day. So, I told my dad how we needed a more serious weapon for the rabbits. He said it was okay, but we had to be careful. We now had another problem: who could we get that was really dumb enough to shoot the thing?

The answer came in through the door as we sat there. Sure enough, in walked Leroy. We told him, "Leroy, with your help, tonight we can take with us a serious weapon." Of course, he had no idea what that was.

So he asked, "What's a serious weapon?"

We told him it was a shotgun. "A weapon that could kill anything in the desert."

His reply was, "Man, I ain't gonna shoot nothing like that and take the life of those animals. I'll be seeing their hants," (White people deal with ghosts, but Blacks call them hants), "and will be haunted for the rest of my life. Ghosts of rabbits, ghosts of lizards, birds and frogs will continue to haunt me forever. When I get to heaven who do you think will be sitting next to Jesus? The hants of all these animals. Then I will have to answer to Jesus."

We were shocked. This wasn't Leroy, where did he get this logic? This wasn't the way he was supposed to respond. Something had snapped back right in his head and for a moment he was rational, logical and sane. We explained to him that he never complained about the hants of any animals when he was taking their lives with slingshots and a bow and arrows. What about all the rabbits he had eaten and the quails? He never complained when they were on his plate smothered in gravy. We finally convinced him that he would be putting food in the mouths of our families and he would be upholding the honor of all the Nightriders. All the little Black Zorros and Robin Hoods in the world would someday honor him for being the pioneer among us to shoot a shotgun. We even told him that he would one day be recognized in Black history as, "The One." I told him to look at himself as a human resource for benevolence. He didn't know what that meant, but since it sounded good he agreed. I also convinced him that no hants would bother him and when he got to heaven the animals wouldn't hold it against him.

Now my dad was worried about whom we would get to shoot the gun first. He figured we would have to find someone very dumb to shoot a shotgun, but when he saw us talking to Leroy, he just started laughing hysterically and walked away. He went into the house and I could hear laughter coming from the house, then I heard Mama faintly say, "Po' Leroy."

That night for dinner we had some brother rabbit syrup and biscuits with butter and some bacon slices, and we were all ready to hunt with a more serious weapon. Leroy's house was different. That boy had venison, rice, poke salad, cornbread and food only White people could afford to eat. I think that's why he was such a good athlete. The boy ate well!

Nightfall came and we were ready to hunt with a serious weapon. We took some charcoal and painted our faces like the Indians. You couldn't see it on our little Black faces, but we saw people do it in sports and on the cowboy movies.

We were ready and we went into the desert. Leroy had the shotgun and the first thing we saw wasn't a rabbit. We stopped and got out of the vehicle and followed Leroy. We're all behind him, pushing him on and telling him to go ahead. We got close enough and realized it wasn't a rabbit; it was a skunk: a polecat that is black with a white stripe, a bushy tail, and pees on people. We decided we had to shoot this thing to get over the jitters of the first shot.

So we told Leroy, "Man, you have to shoot the skunk for initiation."

Leroy put the gun up to sight in the skunk, but he kept walking and getting closer and closer. While we're approaching and tenaciously hanging on to Leroy, I'm thinking this skunk is on the defense, but if we continue to get closer, we are the ones that will be on the defense. The skunk was so close that it could now shoot back at us, and like fools, we had followed Leroy right up to the point of no return. Leroy pointed the gun at the skunk and shot. He didn't hit anything and the gun jumped out of his hand and went into the air. He shot the ground all around the skunk, scared the animal and the skunk literally got pissed off, and we got pissed on. We were all in a row behind Leroy, and he was the only one that was fast enough to outrun the spray from the skunk. He took off running and realized that he had left the gun, turned around in mid-air and grabbed the weapon, and still outran the spray. It was like watching a Road Runner cartoon.

The rest of us failed to escape this tidal wave of skunk pee. Leroy was the only one who made it without being cologned. Of course, the wind was in the animal's favor and the skunk peed all over us. When we got back to the car, Leroy was sitting there too dumb to realize he had pulled one over on us.

"Y'all stank!" he said. "Y'all stank bad! What took y'all so long?"

"Thanks to that funny-looking rabbit you pissed off," we retorted, "we got peed on. Now we need to bathe to get rid of this scent."

If looks could kill, Leroy would have died that night. We went down to the river and we took off our fumigated shirts and rolled in the mud. We let it dry then washed it off. We continued the process until we were able to stand the smell of each other.

We had Dad's truck (we all started driving at eleven years old) and later that night we found our first rabbit, and it ran under a bush. Leroy was on him like white on rice. His eyes flaming red with fire as he looked down the barrel and fired from the back of the truck. It lit up the desert, dust went everywhere and it sounded like a cannon going off. We jumped off the truck and ran down where the rabbit was and waited for the dust to clear. We picked the bush up that Leroy had shot from its roots. There the rabbit was with both paws over his ears and looking up at us, as if to say, "What the h-ll!"

The rabbit jumped up and started running through our feet, and we're all trying to kick the rabbit when reality struck me. I thought, *Where is Leroy?* I turned around and he had loaded the shotgun and was ready to shoot again. I knew we were about to lose a foot or two, because once that boy started concentrating you couldn't cause him to lose focus. I knew someone would probably die. The only way we were going to survive was to leap into the back of the truck where Leroy was. Each of us leaped about ten feet and landed in the truck with Leroy. We were screaming at Leroy, telling him not to shoot.

"Okay, okay," said Leroy, "I ain't gonna shoot if y'all don't want me to."

We thought, *Wow, man, that was a close call.* DJ then started jumping up and down and that's when we realized the rabbit was in the truck with us. He was shaking and I could just hear him thinking to himself, Lord, they done gave a serious weapon to a maniac. He must have thought, What is wrong with all you little Black Zorros?

The poor rabbit jumped out of the truck knowing that the desert would never again be safe as long as a serious weapon was in the hands of Leroy and the Nightriders.

There were two groups in the Toe that didn't want to see a weapon in the hand of a Black man: they were White folk and rabbits. That night we all got the nerves to shoot the shotgun, and we killed eleven rabbits and brought them home and gave them away.

Leroy (a.k.a. Jake, Dumpy, Dumb Dumpy, Fox and Jethro) was so athletic that he would often do superhuman stunts. We knew he was very special but we would never tell him, because we didn't want him to find out. If he would have found out, it would have gone to his head, and there was lots of room in his head for pride, not because it was big, but because it was empty.

I remember one time he showed off his speed. You have to understand that Leroy didn't have the body of Hercules or Atlas. None of us were fat, but we were all lean. Leroy was no different than the rest of us; he was just like a normal kid with a few exceptions. He had big feet, ashy legs, red hair, and an empty head, but other than that he looked normal. Every once in a while we would have to hold him down and grease his ashy legs with some lord or fatback, put some Dixie Peach on his head, comb his hair and slap some lip chap on his lips, but other than that he didn't look too bad except for his nappy red hair. He had red hair and it was so bad that he could bend a stainless steel Afro fork. My hair was a dirty brown and that is why we were often mistaken for each other. One thing I can say about Leroy is that his heart was filled with compassion even though his head was empty. If his head would have been as full of wisdom as his heart was filled with compassion, he would have been a genius. I loved him with all my heart and he was the type to give you all he had: on the field and off the field.

One time we were spending the night over at Leroy's house. It was time for us to go to bed and we were afraid of the dark. Technology had entered the Toe and we had electricity. Sometimes it seemed that the electricity took its time getting to the bulb, but slowly it made it. I mean almost instant light. All you had to do was pull the switch and the room lit up. Kinda like the creation, when God said let there be light and it was. We figured that God created Leroy to have something faster than light. After God had made intelligence, knowledge and understanding, He decided to make something dumb or dumber than dumb, so God made Leroy.

When God made some of them boys in the Toe He must have gone to lunch right before He put in their brain, and when He returned He forgot they weren't finished, and pulled them off the assembly line.

We were spending the night and telling Leroy that he was supposed to be hospitable. Of course, we had to explain to him what that word meant. If we wanted a mayonnaise, bean or syrup sandwich, he was supposed to get it for the guest. We convinced him that he was supposed to treat us well as company. Frank called it hostiltality, but I think he meant hospitality

We told Leroy, you aren't supposed to let people just go into your refrigerator, because that could be embarrassing. We also told him that he was to turn the light off for us after we all got into the bed. We wanted Leroy to oblige us as guests, so we gave him all these instructions for social etiquette. Actually we were scared that if one of us turned the light out, we would have to get back into the bed in the dark. Man, you had to be careful around these guys, because some of them were real sex maniacs, and you never knew what you would be jumping on in the dark.

I know for a fact some of the chickens were incredibly close to some of these guys. If you went to their house, and you hadn't seen them for a while and you embraced them, man, those hens would attack you out of pure jealousy.

So we told Leroy, since you're on the floor with your pallet, why don't you turn the light out?

We had talked him into sleeping on the floor and giving us the bed. If he turned the light out and got on the pallet, he wouldn't have to worry about the perverts in the bed. Leroy agreed, to our surprise. We thought he would turn the light off and freeze in the dark. We would then jump on him pretending to be hants and frighten him.

Leroy told us, "I'm not afraid of the dark. I do this all the time."

We knew he was afraid of the dark, but what he did, I couldn't believe it. I hadn't seen anything so spectacular since Leford, his older brother, scored seventy-eight points in a basketball game during the "Nigga Bowl" after drinking two pints of Tokay wine and while smoking a pack of cigarettes.

Leroy walked up to the light with the string hanging down. We didn't have light switches at that time. He pulled the string to turn the light off and it flickered once, but Leroy was lying on his pallet before the room got dark! Incredible!

That night, as we lay in the bed, and some of us on the floor, DJ decided to tell us about the future. Whenever he did this we laughed like crazy because some of the things that DJ told us about the future were rather ridiculous. This was 1959 and we lived alienated from the real world and there was only one television in the Toe. Our heroes were all White cowboys with white hats, except Hopalong Cassidy, who sometimes dressed in black and wore a black hat.

Now, as I have said previously, I think DJ was born before his time. DJ said that there were going to be airplanes in the future that would be able to take off like a helicopter and go in any direction. He told us there would be boats that could go so fast that they wouldn't touch the water because there would be air between the water and the boat. The really dim-witted thing that he said contradicted even the Bible. There is a scripture, if I can paraphrase, it says, "the tree is known by his fruit" (Matthew 12:33, KJV), but DJ said there would be fruit trees with multiple kinds of fruit on it. You could buy one tree and get grapefruit, oranges and lemons all from the same tree. He then told us that one day there would be real small movie reels that you could take home and somehow play the movie through the TV. You could stop it and play back whatever scene you wanted to see over again. He said you would be able to go to these places that rented these little movies and rent them real cheap. Now, we were still trying to figure out how the image of people could travel through electrical wires and end up on a television screen.

He claimed that people who could not have children could be able to go to a doctor, who could collect the man sperm and the egg from the woman and unite them together and put them inside another woman and the baby would grow. She would be able to carry someone else's child.

We thought this was ridiculous, because there were no eggs inside of a woman, maybe chickens, but not women.

The most bizarre thing that DJ told us was that one day lenses from glasses would be made so small that you could just stick the lens on your eyeball, and you wouldn't need a frame. We knew this was unreasonable, because you would have to have some type of glue to make it stick to a person's eyeball, and if you had to do that, you couldn't see through the glue and it would irritate your eyes so that you would go blind.

He also said movie stars would soon be replaced by cartoon people. When we asked him what he meant, he said that cartoon people would one day look so real that they would no longer have to use real people in movies. The last thing I remember DJ saying was that one day a man could be changed into woman, and a woman could be changed to a man. DJ called it "a sex exchange."

It was about three a.m. when we fell asleep and since no one peed in the bed we slept comfortably. We enjoyed that night with Leroy and there were many more.

DJ (Hick) was weird and hardly ever wore shoes and his feet showed it. You could see where he had stomped his big toe many times. Sometimes when we went to the store barefooted we would have to run from bush to bush and stick our feet underneath the shade to cool them off. Sometimes, we hopped on one foot until it got hot, then we switched to the other foot for a while. DJ would just keep walking with them alligator feet and would be at the store waiting for us, sitting there eating a MoonPie and drinking a RC Cola. The bottom of his foot was like leather.

One of the things we did was to get these signal lights (flares) that had been thrown from the train onto the tracks, and they were made to burn in bad weather. We would try everything we could to put out the flame once they were lit. We would pour water on them, pee on them, and even beat them with sticks, but they just kept burning. Of course, when D.J. peed on the flares it seemed that the flame flared up as if someone had thrown gasoline on the fire. Maybe it was his diet, but that has remained a mystery to this day. We have always known he was full of gas, but that should not have affected his urine. DJ could walk over to a flare and put his barefoot on it and smother it out. The boy would pivot on the flare like in basketball. He would, afterwards, hold his foot up and knock off what little particles were stuck to his foot. It would only leave a little black spot on the bottom of his foot. You couldn't see it, because even the bottom of his feet was black.

DJ never had a lot. His grandmother had taken care of him and his sister. It was an act of godliness. DJ would find shoes in garbage cans or down at the dump. If they were too little he would cut the toes off so he could get his foot inside. DJ's shoes, most of time, wouldn't match. So, it wasn't unusual to see him walking with one shoe different from the other. He would have a boot on one foot and a tennis shoe on the other. If he found a shoe he liked, he would tie it to his waist until he would find another to his liking. When he found another shoe, whether it matched or not, he would put them on. Certain shoes became a match to DJ, even though they were different to the world.

DJ mismatched a pair of shoes on purpose because of his mindset. If he was wearing a tennis shoe and a sandal, he considered that a set. So, whenever you saw him with that particular tennis shoe on, you knew the sandal would be on the other foot.

One day we decided to add on to one of our marathon football games. We would play for days and would continue the score until the end of the month. This particular day we had chosen our team and it was always the hill against the valley. We had chosen our players, but DJ was late, so when he finally showed up, we didn't pay too much attention to him, but noticed that he had on some really neat black and white shoes with the tongue flopped over the front of the shoe. You know, the kind that White folk wore. The odd thing about those shoes was that they matched. He had finally found a set that matched.

We took old pillows and cut a hole in the center and pulled it over our heads, followed by a sweatshirt, and those were our shoulder pads. If we didn't have an old pillow we would just stuff our shirts with cotton or old rags. We tied the bottom of our pant legs after stuffing them with cotton from the fields or some old rags, and we were ready to play.

The game started and the valley was doing pretty good. Cleo was handling the ball well, but on that day Leroy had to play a little while with each team, because he didn't live in the valley or on the hill. He lived right at the cutoff mark. Actually, having Leroy play only on one side would have made the game lopsided. I guess living on the cutoff mark and playing on both teams entitled Leroy to say he never lost a game; of course, on the other hand, you could say he always lost.

He was being kept in check during the game, because we would knock him around a little bit and take some cheap shots when he wasn't looking. We would tackle him and knock him into a bush or some old junk car. It would take about three of us to get him down, and when we did we would steal his shoe off his foot while he was under the pile and hide it under our shirt. Everyone in the Toe knew that if you really needed to get somewhere in a hurry you took off your shoes. So, no one was allowed to play barefooted because it would give him an advantage. Leroy would sit out a play or two trying to find his shoe, then it would mysteriously show up again, right there in the middle of the field.

Leroy was as good as the quarterback made him. If the quarterback was dumb and didn't use him properly, then Leroy had no game. If he were smart, like me, I would use him almost every play and watch him destroy the other team. He was a one-man wrecking crew and at the same time he was grace and sweetness in motion. He ran like the wind and could stop on a dime. He was the epitome of action.

DJ went to the hill side, because he lived right next to the ditch and the hill needed another player, because Frank was acting like a nut, or shall I say, being himself, threatening to take his ball and wanting to fight after every play. Half the time the ball didn't belong to him, so we had to tell him, "Nigga, please, put the ball down, because it's not yours."

After watching Frank I said to the others, "This Negro need to be replaced, 'cause he ain't going to act right."

The only way I could control Frank was to be on his team. He would listen to me if I was on his team, but not as an opponent. So for peace's sake Frank came on our team and DJ went to the hill. I still had to convince Frank that he couldn't take the ball if it didn't belong to him.

Like a light switch going on, Frank thought aloud, *Oh, that's right, I can't take the ball if it's not mine.*

We had a good game going on. Frank's mom, Mrs. Etta, brought us some teacakes and Kool-Aid and we hadn't even gotten to halftime. We were hitting hard that day, and I mean head to chest. We would hit each other so hard that the numbers we wrote on our shirts would be erased and would appear on the forehead of the tackler.

Now, for some reason, they kept giving DJ the ball, and it was hard to keep him from driving those few extra yards. It seemed that his shoes had that extra traction. One time we gang-tackled the boy, and they had to carry him back to the huddle. When we got back to our huddle, I noticed that each person was bleeding. Cleo's arm, Frank's legs and Morris's elbows were bleeding. Morris was a new kid who had moved to the Toe. He was the nice kid who was in each of us, but he always exhibited this nice person outwardly.

When I brought it to their attention that we were all bleeding, they reminded me that I wasn't excluded, because blood was all over me. I checked each person out and found that we all had little holes all over us. The holes appeared as puncture marks, but they were in a pattern.

I called time-out, and we checked everybody's shoes. Now, most of us had on a decent pair of U.S. Keds. We couldn't afford those new shoes called Converse All-Stars. Some of us had wire as shoestring, but the wire was bent down so it couldn't hurt anyone.

When I got to DJ I found the problem. He had gone down to the rummage sale and picked up a dime pair of shoes; the only problem was they were golf shoes. They had little spikes underneath, and DJ had left his mark on all of us, including some of his own players.

We made DJ take his shoes off, because we were being punctured. Now, this only led to the hill catching up with us, because there was no way we could catch DJ if he was barefooted. The boy was unstoppable. He scored five touchdowns and kicked five extra points and six field goals. All this was done barefooted after we made him take the shoes off.

DJ was the first human being in this world who kicked barefooted. For our extra points, we would go over to the telephone poles and kick the ball over the wire that connected the poles. If the electric lines were an inconvenience, we would find us a tree close by and kick the ball over it. At the end of the day, the score was valley with 406, to the hill's 402. We wrote down the score, so when we played again we would start from those figures.

After the summer we went down to the cotton field and had to pick cotton for our lunch money for school. While we were there DJ did his out-of-the-mind thing. Just out of the clear blue sky DJ would do something stupid for no reason at all. It was like his mind would go back in time and whatever he was thinking about he would react to it. Sometimes we would have to shake him to bring him back from fantasy land.

Cleo and I were having a normal conversation after we had weighed our cotton sacks and were standing near a ditch bank. We were discussing things like how many planets are there in Texas, is the horse of Troy really the biggest horse in the world, and is Texas bigger than America?

Leroy told us that in the story of Helen of Troy, they rode the horse to the gate of the city. They then cut the horse open and put the people inside.

Now while we are talking, DJ came up to Cleo and hit him in the jaw. Cleo fell down into the ditch holding his jaw.

Cleo got up and shouted, “Boy, why you hit me?”

DJ got this empty look on his face and said, “I don’t know, I really don’t know.”

I told Cleo, “Maybe somewhere in his past life you pissed him off, and he finally realized it was you.”

Cleo walked slowly over to him and then hit DJ and knocked him into the ditch. He was on DJ like a fly on honey. We were stunned.

We kept saying to each other, “Cleo is nonviolent.”

DJ started yelling, “Why don’t y’all tell him that he’s nonviolent?”

So we pulled Cleo off of DJ and told him, “Cleo, you’re nonviolent.”

DJ got up and came over and he yelled, “Why did you hit me?”

Cleo looked at him and said sarcastically, “I don’t know, I really don’t know!”

We all returned to work and decided this would be our last sack of cotton for the day. What that meant was we were to load it up. When I say, “load it up,” I mean with whatever you could get into the sack without it being noticeable when you weighed in. We put our sweaters, jackets, and clods of dirt, boots, hats and caps inside that last sack of cotton. By the time we stuffed half our clothes in our sacks, we were near naked.

Now it took a dumb person to take this sack up to the scales, so, of course, we selected Leroy to do it. On top of the trailer a person was packing the cotton down with his feet and checking for debris or contraband. The person for the day was Len. Len was older than the rest of us and was DJ’s kinfolk and the boy had big feet. It must have been something that ran in the family. History has it that on one occasion Len got scared and he ran on water. I know Len wasn't that spiritual so it must have been the size of his feet.

While Leroy was taking the sack of cotton up to the trailer and emptying it out, we were supposed to distract Len in some way. We would yell up to him and ask him something about his girlfriend or pretend to be fighting among ourselves. The one thing that caught his attention was when we yelled, "Snake!"

Now Gootee, of course, had to put a turd in his sack. When Len stepped on it, he realized what it was and started yelling, "Who put do-do in the sack?"

Everyone responded, "Guess!"

The first name that came out of Len's mouth was, "Gootee!"

Len jumped off the trailer and started chasing after Gootee and caught him. Can you believe it? We are talking about the boy who was faster than the do-do bug. The reason this was made possible is because Gootee couldn't stop laughing. Len grabbed Gootee around the collar and lifted him off the ground. Gootee's feet were dangling above the ground as Len reached back like he was going to hit Gootee. Gootee stopped laughing as Len balled up his fist and was about to throw a punch. Gootee came to himself and hit Len seven times before Len knew what happened. It was like watching Popeye and Brutus fight after Popeye had his spinach. Len was stunned by Gootee's quickness, and he dropped the boy on the ground and Gootee took off running. It was about five seconds later the boy was out of sight.

After the scuffle between Len and Gootee had taken place, I went over to where it happened and found Gootee's glasses on the ground. While I'm holding them up thinking how nice it would be not to have to wear glasses, DJ came over and interceded.

"I know what you're thinking," he stated, "but one day those lenses will be so small you can just stick the lens on your eyeball."

Again I shot him down with the theory of the glue between the lenses, and the eyeball would be too irritable.

DJ walked away examining the glasses, then he replied, "Maybe you won't need glue. They could possibly stick to the eye without it."

We all started laughing and went to gather up our clothes from Leroy who had emptied our sacks into the trailer and had thrown our clothes over behind the trailer while Len and Gootee were fighting.

DJ was still sitting on the ditch bank examining the glasses when Cleo walked up to him, and again hit him in the jaw. Cleo done already whooped him once that day, and we all thought it was over. DJ rolled down the ditch bank, still holding onto Gootee's glasses. Cleo wiped his hands together as if to say, take that!

DJ came out of the ditch holding his jaw and asking Cleo, "Why did you hit me? Boy, is you going berserk?"

Cleo was not dumb. He answered like a stuck record, "I don't know, I don't know, I don't know."

I thought after Cleo hit DJ that DJ would get angry, but instead DJ came up with another theory. Perhaps Cleo had knocked the idea into his head.

"Maybe the moisture from the eyeball would hold the lens on," he shouted.

"What are you talking about?" I replied.

"Maybe the lens could have contact with the eyes and stick to them," retorted DJ. "Perhaps they could call them contact lenses?"

Again we cracked up, because you would have to be crying twenty-four-seven for that to happen.

Finally, Len returned to the trailer and made us give back half the money for the last sack load or he would tell our mamas. We did and that was probably our first lesson on integrity.

It was time to go hunting and this time I was going with crazy Gootee. My Uncle Buddy was Gootee's stepfather, but it was amazing how much they looked alike and acted alike. Uncle Buddy was full of tall tales. He warned us to be careful of the joint snake. We had no idea what he was talking about, so, of course, he explained. He told us that there was a snake in the desert called the "joint snake," and the reason he was called that was because if you hit it or shot at it, it would fall apart into many small pieces. So when you see this snake in all these pieces, you would think you did it when you hit him or shot him. He said when you leave all the pieces it would come back together and the snake would go on about his business. He said the only way to kill the snake was to hide or destroy one of the pieces, but there was no way I was going to put my hand on any piece of a joint snake. What would happen if I took a piece and placed it in my pocket, and forgot to take the piece out of my pocket, and it followed me home and came together in my pocket? As far as I was concerned, if we saw this snake he would have no problem with me.

Uncle Buddy told us that he was hunting one day and he saw this tepee. Yes, I mean an Indian's tent house. I mean Indian, like Cochise, Geronimo or Crazy Horse. He said he saw a little tent with a snake's head sticking out of the top and then he realized it was a rattlesnake coiled up five feet high. Now normally I wouldn't believe this if anyone else had told me, but this man was a deacon in the church, so I figured he wouldn't lie. Then he said that on one of his famous hunting trips he heard a noise in the sky and when he looked up he saw an airplane pulling two cars. That was when I realized that church folk don't always tell the truth.

We used Uncle Buddy to mediate for us when we would have an argument about who shot what. You see, Gootee would always claim that he shot everything. When we got home we would take the rabbit or whatever it was to Uncle Buddy and he would decide who really shot it.

We went hunting, and honestly, I don't know why I hunted with that boy. Huey was with us and he would decide once in a while, but Huey was rather biased, because once he learned that Gootee had peed on his head, and that do-do bugs didn't really exist, he would give me the benefit of the doubt. Gootee had done so many things to Huey, so I knew Huey would always make the decision in my favor.

Huey didn't have a gun, but agreed he wouldn't take his shoes off and catch the rabbits, but would allow us the opportunity to shoot them. We knew that if Huey was involved in the hunting and he was barefooted, we didn't have a chance. I know the rabbits were pleased that we elected to keep Huey out of our contest, and he had conceded to our agreement. Huey was just walking and singing. Huey could sing but be couldn't talk for stuttering. Sometimes when he had something to say that was urgent we would tell him to sing it.

We finally saw a dove in a tree and Gootee told me to get closer, but as I started to get closer he fired his weapon. I should have known not to trust this boy, but I forgot. I looked up to see if the bird was still there and it was. I took a careful aim and as I pulled the trigger I heard Gootee shoot at the same time. This time the bird fell out of the tree. I was already in the lower brush, so I retrieved it and brought it out to the clearing.

Gootee shouted, "You see that, man, and I took him out with a single shot."

Yes, Gootee was trying to take credit for the bird I had just shot.

I retorted, "If you touch my bird I will shoot your arm off!"

He started arguing that he had shot the bird. When we asked Huey, he stuttered so much we both told him to shut up. We decided that Uncle Buddy would decide.

Then a jackrabbit jumped up and our imaginations went wild. Man, all we could see was rabbit in gravy, rabbit with rice and biscuits, fried rabbit and barbecued rabbit. The rabbit was running like something was wrong with his leg and we hadn't even shot at 'em. We started unloading on that sucker. I shot three times with the shotgun after reloading and Gootee reloaded his "semi-automatic 22-caliber rifle" after shooting nineteen times.

After the dust cleared the rabbit was still standing. The rabbit just stood there vacillating like a tree branch in the wind. He started to run and then he stopped and fell over dead. Huey ran over to the rabbit and kicked him in the head, like it was really necessary. I mean, if Huey kicked you in the head with them alligator feet, you would probably die twice.

Gootee and I both grabbed for the rabbit and the fight was on. I don't know why we didn't shoot each other, but the first thing we did was put the guns down and start fighting. Well, Huey broke us up and told us that he had made the decision and as far as he was concerned he was the one who had killed the rabbit when he kicked it. He was stuttering and trying to tell us that we told him to kick the rabbit so the rabbit was his.

He said, "This ra-rab-bi-bit rabbit, is-is-is mi-mi-mine, cause me-I ki-kicked it de-dead."

Right away, Gootee and I let that boy know, "Fool, this ain't even under arbitration and if it was you wouldn't be a participant."

We took the dove and the rabbit to Uncle Buddy to let him make the decision. Of course, he was sitting in this big lawn chair that he made and was drinking a big glass of Kool-Aid or White Water soda and snacking on a bowl of turnip greens. Uncle Buddy was a fat jolly person and he reminded me of a Black Santa Claus without the beard and presents.

The first words out of his mouth were, "Uh uh uuh, ain't nobody hit this dove, y'all must have scared him to death."

Sure enough, the bird didn't have a single hole in him or any sign of blood to show he had been shot. Then we checked the rabbit closely and there weren't any holes in him, but one leg was missing. Immediately we both claimed to have shot the rabbit's leg off and he died from shock.

Uncle Buddy said, "This rabbit had been missing a leg for a month and y'all ought to be 'shamed of yourselves for shooting a three-legged rabbit." He belted his decision, "This little dove ain't gonna feed nobody so y'all might as well give him to me as a decision-making fee and if anyone should get the rabbit it should be Huey, because he did kick him in the head."

"Huey!" we both yelled in unison. "He ain't even gotta gun!"

"Yeah, but look at his head, it was the blow to the head that finished him off," replied Unc.

This man, my uncle, I'm talking my blood relative and Gootee's father, took our rabbit and gave him to crazy stuttering Huey. Now, I'm thinking to myself, as Huey is walking away with my rabbit, *I'm glad Gootee peed on ya head.*

CHAPTER EIGHT

Tragedies

I believe that to really measure love in the heart of a person you must first measure the God in them. I feel love is more than the sharing of laughter and good times, but having cried together and having endured trials and tribulations of life together. It is the adversities in life that truly bring out the love and true friendship in people.

We were told, as we grew up, that all activities had to cease on Sundays. We were not allowed to go swimming in the canal on Sunday or play sports. One day while we were at church my cousin Johnny decided that he was going swimming. The next thing we knew an ambulance came to the Toe and went screaming toward the canal. I knew it must have been someone drunk who had driven into the canal, but we were all saddened when we were told that Johnny had gone swimming and had drowned. This only confirmed our fear about doing anything on Sunday, other than going to church. The sadness of this occasion permeated throughout the community and the fear that came over our parents lasted for months. None of us were allowed to go near the canal for the next six months.

Another terrible tragedy was when Cleo and Jerry's mom passed away in the night after being sick for a while. I cried not for myself but for my friends who had lost a dear mother. It was good to be in the Toe, because though they had lost a mother, they were not motherless. Mother Hall was a lady who was in the church and she had a heart of gold. She personified kindness and shared herself according to God's will. She came from Tucson to help out, and the Toe family also did what they could to help. Mother Hall spent her life trying to be the mother who they had lost. I could not imagine what it would be like to lose a parent.

It seemed that every person I knew who went into a hospital never came out alive. My sister Mary and I were the only ones, so far.

Another tragedy occurred when Mutt shot Zelma, his wife and my cousin. Mutt was never a mean or bad person. That was evident when Frank stole his money. He really wasn't going to hurt us, but we did deserve punishment for being an accessory to the crime, which Frank had committed, and we did chew some of the bubble gum. We knew that money wasn't just coming out of the ground. We knew Frank had taken someone's money, we just didn't know whose.

Again the details were kept from us as children. She was a very beautiful lady, and I liked her a lot. We were at school when this happened, and they got all of us Toe children out of class and kept us together. We had gone on a trip earlier that day and we saw a car along the side of the road with the sheriff deputies around it, but we had no idea what had happened. The school sent us home later that day, and that's when we learned that Zelma was dead.

The Toe was split and the schisms lasted for years in the hearts of many. We all attended Zelma's funeral and it was very sad. The church was much too small to accommodate the people. The sheriff deputies were there and anger filled the air. Zelma had been very nice to me as a child. I still remember her face as I gazed into her casket, thinking to myself, *Why, why did she have to die?*

Even in death she was still very beautiful. I cried my heart out and tried hard to understand why she was chosen by the Death Angel. I would find myself asking God, "Why Zelma?" I have since learned that God has given us free will, and what we do with the free will is not always God's will. Life is too brief and precious not to make the best of it.

It is written, "*As for man, his days are as grass: as a flower of the field, so he flourisheth. For the wind passeth over it, and it is gone; and the place thereof shall know it no more... For all flesh is as grass, and all the glory of man as the flower of grass. The grass withereth, and the flower thereof falleth away*" (Psalms 103:15-16, 1pet 1:24).

The next tragedy that came upon us was when we lost Luke. We don't know the facts that caused Luke's death, but there was a rumor that was most popular. One night Luke came home and his sister Sarah and her husband, Don, were visiting the Toe. Don had seen something about Luke that bothered him, so he asked Luke to go home with him, but Luke said everything was okay. Sarah, Luke's sister, was a very quiet and beautiful person, and apparently hadn't discerned the presence of the Death Angel, who was visiting Luke that night. Again Don felt compelled to get Luke out of the Toe that night, but again he was unable to convince Luke to go with him. It was about one a.m. when Don and Sarah went home. On the way home Don mentioned to Sarah how they should have convinced Luke to come with them, because something just wasn't right. Later on in the early morning Pastor Hopkins came to their home with the news that Luke had been shot to death.

Luke was allegedly involved in an incident of some sort, but the owner of the establishment, being White, shot him with a shotgun as he turned to leave the store. No one knows why Luke was in a store at three a.m. that should have been closed at sundown. Neither is it clear how they both found themselves in the store having a conversation at three in the morning. The owner knew Luke, and he stated Luke had a weapon and was fiddling around in the store with the intent to rob the store. The owner said he had advised Luke that he knew what he was up to, and advised him not to try it. No one knows what spark ignited the fire, but the owner grabbed his shotgun and shot him at close range.

It was just another opportunity for a White man to shoot a Black man and get away with it. My thoughts are you should never give any man the legal right or excuse to shoot you, because he just might do it. When the Death Angel knocks, someone has to answer.

My nephew would let Luke cut his hair and Luke had touched his life like he had many of ours. Tater would wake up at night talking about Luke and how he dreamed about him. It took almost six months before he could sleep normally.

It was the loss of lives in the Toe that brought us even closer together. When someone lost a sister or brother, father or mother, we all lost a sister or brother or father or mother. When a parent lost a son or daughter, all the parents in the Toe lost a son or daughter. The life we all lived in that little community was full of joy, but there were times when our hearts would sink to the bottomless pit of sorrow.

It was during those times that I realized that the Death Angel had passed through the Toe and taken our loved ones. I could never understand the selective process of the Death Angel.

When Cleo asked me the question, "Why do good people die and bad people go on living?" I could not answer him.

He then asked, "Why do bad things happen to good people?" and again, I couldn't answer his question, so I just cried.

The tears continued to flow when he asked, "Why did God take my mama and let the wino live?"

These were questions to which I had not found the answer at that time in life. I had a hard time trying to explain to Jerry about his mother being with God, but I think what I said did help.

I let him know that, "She was a saint of God and that death was not a period that ends the sentence of life, but a comma that shows continuation."

I remembered the words of my dear mother who said, "The God that gives both love and life can surely take it away."

I am reminded of the words of a song:

When death has come and taken our loved one
It leaves our home so lonely and drear
But then do we wonder why others prosper
Living so wicked year after year.
Further along we'll know all about it
Further along we'll understand why
Cheer up, my brother, live in the sunshine
We'll understand it all, by and by

We all had a fear of going to the hospital, because we felt no one ever returned. The reason for this was rather simple and I had figured it out. It seemed that no one went to the hospital unless they were dying. Many could not afford treatment or doctors because we were too poor. When someone went to the hospital it was to die. If God would not heal us, then there was nothing the doctors could do. If we did go to the hospital and came out, God got the glory.

When Cleo had to go to the hospital we all knew it was over for him. We all went down to the walnut trees and cried because we knew that everyone who went into the hospital never came out alive. We thought it was over, but God heard our prayers and brought him back.

Cleo had a knot on his penis, which resulted from not being circumcised. We figured the doctor would have to cut his penis off. If this was the outcome we knew he would not want to live without a penis. He would not be able to be a real challenger in our frequent peeing contests. Poor Cleo would be penisless.

You must understand that little boys take part in various games that only boys know about. We had guys who could walk almost a quarter of a mile while peeing on the ground. The event covered two categories: one, you had to stand in one spot and see how far you could pee, and the other was you had a starting point and you tried to cover as much ground as possible before you stop peeing. It remained to this day that no one could out-pee DJ. He actually peed twenty feet from a standing position, and walked a quarter of mile (second category), and set the Rillito Peeing Record.

We were really happy that Cleo didn't die, because to lose someone that close would be like someone reaching inside your body and pulling out a piece of you, never to replace it. We had enough death and God finally sent the Death Angel somewhere else.

A strange thing happened when the boy went into the hospital. We believed that there was negative and positive reciprocal force: when you give up something good then something bad will take its place, and when you give up something bad, something good will happen to you. It was like having a trade-off and that was what happened to Cleo. He went into the hospital to have the knot taken off his penis, now that was a good thing. The bad thing was when they operated on him, apparently the negative force went through the utensils that were used and then into his fingers. In other words, the evil that would have been associated with his penis went to his fingers.

The boy came out of the hospital a thief. This was a person who never stole anything in his life, but after the removal of the knot on his penis he became a thief. I mean an authentic rogue. He was so good at stealing that sometimes he didn't realize he had stolen certain things. He would walk inside of people's houses and walk out with dolls, rings, bracelets, earrings, necklaces and so on. Then later on in life he would walk into people's houses and walk out with larger items. Things like teddy bears, hula hoops and chairs.

Sometimes we would have to yell at him, "Boy, put that chair back, drop the dog, or put that chicken down!"

He would go to the store to buy a Big Hunk or a Zero candy bar and come out with a loaf of bread, a can of Spam or Vienna sausage. We thanked God for not letting Cleo wake up dead.

One day a great mystery came over the Toe. It seemed that all the older guys of a certain age all left the Toe for a while. I wondered what was going on so I went to Uncle Buddy to try and tap into his great wisdom. If he wasn't talking in parables, he talked in King James rhetoric. He would say things like, "Goest thou thine own way and be thou cool." Uncle tried to talk in parables because he was a deacon, but I seldom understood him. Instead of just telling you something, every answer had to have a story.

He said, "There was a girl once who was so skinny that she swallowed an olive and most of the young men left town."

Now I could not figure this out for the death of me. Then it hit! The rumor was that Josie had gotten pregnant, so that was why everybody over eighteen left town. I don't know why Unc just didn't say Josie was pregnant and the suspects all left town. We started thinking, *Man, she must have messed around with a lot of dudes*. Then Frank and Lee said we needed to have an emergency Nightrider meeting, because something important had come up.

That night we had our meeting around a burning tire over near the cottonwood tree. Frank and Lee said they had to confess to something. Right away everybody said, "Oh no, Frank done killed somebody!" Others said, "No, the people in the white clothes and straightjackets are probably coming for Lee."

Frank belted, "No! It's worse than that!"

Lee confirmed it when he said, "It sure is!"

By now we didn't have a clue what they were talking about and we were begging them to tell us. Then they let us have it. Frank and Lee both said they had kissed Josie!

Frank said, "I kissed her on the cheek."

Immediately we straightened him out: "Fool, you can't get nobody pregnant by kissing them on the cheek."

Lee then dropped the hammer on us. He said, "I kissed her on the lips and she stuck her tongue in my mouth."

Right away we knew this was very serious, because we knew that might have gotten her pregnant. It seemed that when folk kissed like that the girl always came up pregnant.

We encouraged Frank to stay, but we told Lee he better leave town. The boy was so scared he hid for a month, until one day I went and asked Josie if Lee had gotten her pregnant.

She told me, "Lee don't know how to get nobody pregnant." Then she said, "I'm just a little pregnant anyway."

I could never figure out how someone could be a little pregnant. Josie was the only person I knew who could be a little pregnant, and then get more pregnant as time went on.

The Toe was like a Peton Place, lots of them kids coming up after us, who were born in the Toe, didn't even know who their daddy was. We could be playing sports and somebody would do something really spectacular and some old dude would say something like, "That's my boy," and everyone would get quiet and turn to see who it was. You know like that E.F. Hutton commercial. Then they would be looking to see if he favored you in some way. I mean, they would look at your feet then his feet, your head then his head, and this would go on with other parts of your body until they would conclude if it was possible for him to be your daddy or not.

I remember this girl who was about twelve years old telling me that one day she was going to marry a certain boy.

Her daddy said, "No way, you ain't gonna marry him."

When she asked him why, he told her that when he was a lad he sowed his seed among the wild weeds. Now what he was trying to say was he was running around tipping and dipping. What that meant was he was lying around and sleeping around with other women. Women like Bebe. He then told her that the boy could be her brother. Man, isn't that a terrible thing to tell your daughter about the person she wanted to marry?

I told that girl, "Go tell your mama what he said."

The girl was crying when she went to her mother who was sitting on the couch.

Her mom asked, "What's wrong?"

"Daddy said I couldn't marry my boyfriend, because he could be my brother," she responded.

I thought to myself, *Dammnn! She really told her mama!*

Her mom was heated and I could see the temperature rising; sweat started dropping down her face and her hair started getting nappy. The woman got so mad even I got scared, just standing there looking at her.

Then her mama bellowed, "Child, you go ahead and marry him, don't listen to what that man tells you. Hell, he ain't your daddy no way."

The Toe benefitted when Josie got pregnant, because all them boys who left town went and joined the Army, Navy, Air Force or the Marines. It was like when Rome was persecuting the Christians and they scattered abroad. It benefitted the gospel in being carried abroad. The Toe started to spread her wings all because of Josie and a couple of others.

We were so happy that Lee didn't have to leave town nor did they even consider him a suspect in this case. We later learned that it took more than a kiss to get a girl pregnant, but a kiss was usually what started it. We decided kissing was out for us boys, especially the tongue thing, which was a no-no!

One weekend we had worked in the cotton fields and we had about twenty dollars. We had gotten a raise and made six dollars a day chopping cotton and we usually ate a dollar's worth of food each day. The first thing we did when we got to town was to get all one dollar bills, so it looked like we had a lot of money to the city boys. Now, of course, this money would be put into a brand new Zorro or Lone Ranger wallet.

One day we went over to Syl's house and he was the type of brother it was hard to love. He was always playing practical jokes on people. His jokes were not like Gootee's, because his jokes could seriously hurt somebody. If we all weren't in love with Lena, his sister, we would have killed Syl long time ago. Lena kept that nigga alive, and she didn't even know it.

I only loved Syl because I had to; other than that; I would have put him out of his misery. If I hadn't liked Lena so much, I think terminating Syl would have made me popular. He was the type of person you would like to trick into going to a KKK meeting and then leave him there, or tie him to the train tracks, get a bag of popcorn and Kool-Aid, and watch the train run over him. One thing about Syl, if you could go deep enough you could find compassion, but it was real deep inside him. Syl was very generous and I think if you looked hard enough you could find some other reason to love him besides him having Lena as a sister and being born into a good family.

Syl had all kinds of vices. I mean, he smoked five different kinds of cigarettes. One time he gave me a Kool cigarette, and I took one draw and it was like biting into a frozen lemon. They had to pour warm water on my lips to get them back to normal again. He smoked Camel cigarettes and that was like eating nicotine out of bowl with a spoon. He walked around with five different brands of cigarettes on him and he would never smoke the same brand cigarette twice. I'm not talking about somebody that was twenty-one years old. This boy was only twelve years old and he would suck on cigarettes like the rest of us did LifeSavers and Jawbreakers.

There was a Camel commercial that advertised that people would walk a mile for a Camel. There was also a Chesterfield commercial that said Chesterfields wanted to satisfy. Syl told us that when he took a girl out on his motor scooter he would pull out a Camel and a Chesterfield cigarette, and ask them if they were going to be like a Camel and walk a mile back to the house or like the Chesterfield and satisfy. He was only twelve and the only sexual encounter he ever had was watching the dogs and the other domestic animals mate. There was a rumor about him and some chickens, but we never thought much of it.

Syl must have started smoking when he was ten and by the time he was thirteen he was winning the soda water drinking contest in the Toe. We would see who could drink a sixteen-ounce soda without bringing it down. Most of us could handle a grape or orange, and we had no trouble with a Delaware Punch. Who ever named that soda should have just called it Delaware, because there was no punch in Delaware Punch. It was like drinking Kool-Aid.

Syl told us he was going to set the record that day by drinking a 32-ounce bottle of soda. Now we figured he had put some Kool-Aid in a 32-ounce bottle and was going to try and trick us. He showed us this paper bag and claimed the soda was in the bag. We started laughing then he pulled out the soda he was going to drink. Man, our eyes got big and folk started gathering around. Syl pulled out of his bag a 32-ounce bottle of Double Cola!

Man, we used Double Cola for cleaning tools, and if your car battery had corrosion on it, we would pour Double Cola on it, and it would clean the battery acid off the cables. You had to wipe it off fast because Double Cola would dissolve the battery cables if you left it on too long. Whenever we got tar stuck on our shoe we would pour Double Cola on it to get the tar off. We would put a couple of drops of Double Cola in the water when we wanted to clean our hands. If you didn't wipe the stuff off of your hands fast enough, you had to walk around a few hours with white hands.

Now, Syl swore he was going to drink this bottle of Double Cola nonstop. Syl took the 32-ounce bottle, opened it with his teeth and drank it all without bringing it down. He didn't waste one drop and when he finished, he belched and licked his lips like he had just finished eating a chicken wing. He then stuck the bottle back into his mouth and started sucking the air out of the bottle until we grabbed it from him in fear that the bottle would explode from the pressure.

When we drank during the soda contest, most of us would have soda running all down our chest and sometimes we would get disqualified. Syl didn't lose a drop so we gave him the winning prize: two MoonPies and twenty cents in change.

Man, that contest broke us, so we had to buy our sodas on credit from Syl's dad. Syl's dad allowed all of us to set up an account with him and buy sodas on credit. The way this started was Syl's father had left him in charge of the sodas, and he was supposed to charge ten cents a soda. We didn't have any money so Syl let us have the sodas on credit. When his father came home and all the sodas were gone, he was so proud of Syl until he asked for the money. When Syl handed him a paper with all our names on it listing our IOU's, he almost fainted. It did teach some of us to be responsible, but others just kept getting farther in debt, because they would never pay their bill.

One day Syl said his dad had given him a bunch of apples and we should try to win them in a shooting contest with our homemade bows and arrows. He put the apples on a fence and we had to shoot them off if we wanted them.

Syl's father had told him to give the apples to the boys in the hood, but he wouldn't tell us. He made us shoot for them like Robin Hood and his Merry Men. Now, we never really cared for Robin Hood, because he wore those tight britches, but Zorro, Cisco Kid and the Lone Ranger, they were the Man.

Syl set up a contest for us to win the apples that he should have given away for free. I told Syl that we should give them away free and distribute them according to intellect, but of course, Leroy got upset and said every time we did that he never got anything. He couldn't understand why they always gave me five to his one. He then wanted to do it according to athletic ability. Right away we all disagreed. We knew if that were the case, he would be walking around with the whole box of apples.

Syl said, "No!"

He was adamant about having the contest. Man, I was so happy, because I knew from the depth of my soul I was the best shot in the Toe. I was so good the boys would call me "deadeye." This was in respect to my awesome accuracy. Syl lined them apples up on that fence fifteen at a time, and I was knocking them off one by one. I was shooting with my eyes closed, shooting behind my back, and apples was falling off the fence simply out of fear. Both my pockets were full, and I was eating apples and still shooting. I told Syl I thought we should conclude the contest and distribute the apples that were left to the boys, that way Leroy would get some and Frank would stop cussing.

Just about the time we were about to conclude this business, DJ came and said he had just invented the "boomerang bow and arrow set." He convinced us that it would be unfair if he didn't at least get a chance to shoot. I knew DJ and he was the type to go around telling people for the rest of our lives that I had won unfairly. I knew him well, and Lee said he even knew the three men who claimed to be the boy's daddy.

We all were curious and wanted to see this bow and arrow invention that he claimed would replace most conventional weapons. DJ walked over to a grassy spot on the ground and unrolled the dirty blanket he was carrying. It looked familiar and I perceived that he had stolen the blanket off of someone's clothesline.

This was the most hideous bow and arrow set that my eyes had ever beheld. The bow was so crooked it went in three directions and was about five feet tall. His bow string was made of wire that he got from burning a car tire. The most amazing thing was the arrow he pulled out of the blanket was about three feet long, and it was shaped like a banana. He claimed it to be "the boomerang arrow," and said it could only be shot by "the boomerang bow."

The boy had flipped. I knew if he kept eating those mesquite beans and eating those unknown desert plants and all that sugar syrup, one day he would go crazy. This was the day and the boy had gone mad. This boy would cut tar off the highway and chew it for gum, and he ate watermelon rinds that had been thrown in the ditch (water canal) by people picnicking upstream. He went everywhere barefooted, and I seen him put out a flare with his bare foot. Finally he had gone berserk.

He gave us a preview of what was going to happen once he shot the arrow. He stated that the arrow, after it had been shot from the boomerang bow, would turn sideways and knock off all the apples, then return to him. Man, we were rolling on the ground laughing so hard we were crying.

He lined up his target and was about to shoot when we realized the arrow was pointing at us.

"Hold it, fool!" we yelled. "Hold it!"

We stopped him and everybody moved to the other side. The boy shot the arrow, and the thing went toward the fence, then turned sideways and knocked thirteen apples off the fence.

We were amazed and happy for DJ. Finally he had invented something that worked. We were jumping up and down, rolling around and cheering DJ for what he had accomplished. We looked around so we could hug him and congratulate him, but DJ had walked away in disgust and was sitting on a five-gallon can angry. We couldn't understand what his problem was.

"What's wrong, DJ?" we asked in unison.

DJ responded, "Ah, man, it did it again."

I said, "You ain't lying, boy, it sure did. Man, you knocked 'em all down!"

Then he yelled, "It didn't work, Codas! It didn't work!"

Not having a clue about what he was insinuating I asked, "DJ, what do you mean it didn't work? You knocked 'em all off the fence."

DJ responded, "The arrow was supposed to knock them off and bring 'em back to me."

Everybody looked at DJ and at the same time said, "Nigga, please!"

It was difficult, but we cheered him up and finally convinced him that his invention was not at all a failure. After all, he had knocked down more apples in one shot than Frank had done all morning.

The next time we found ourselves over to Cleo's house. He wanted to have a soda water skeeting contest. Now, you have to keep in mind we "contested" everything. Every time you looked around we were in some contest. It didn't matter what the situation was; if it was peeing, drinking sodas, shooting arrows, passing gas, skeeting sodas or playing ball, we made a contest of it. We constantly competed against each other in everything.

We shook the sodas really hard and we were skeeting (squirting) sodas at each other. We had gotten the sodas from Cleo's dad's stockpile. You see, he was a contractor and was over the people when they went out to chop or pick cotton on the different farms. Well, we took some sodas, which he had stored and had drank enough to get full. Now it was time to play.

The person who was the least wet was considered the winner. Soda skeeting was an art and there were certain types we did not allow. Double Cola, R.C. and Coke were some of the favorites. Hires root beer was outlawed from any contest because it never lost its fizz. Cleo sneaked in a ringer and was winning no hands down. This boy came out with a soda in a paper bag. Now, we should have known, because when someone conceals anything in a paper bag something is wrong. His soda seemed to have fizz all the time, but ours had lost their fizz after shaking them furiously several times. Everybody tried to figure out what Cleo had, but he wasn't the type to cheat so we kept on playing and getting soaked. Finally I decided after sucking on my shirt that the soda Cleo was using tasted like root beer! So we all jumped him and threw that little sucker on the ground, took his bag and pulled out the mystery soda. We couldn't believe our eyes. Cleo had become like us and he was cheating and had stepped across the ultimate barrier. He was using Hires root beer and everybody knew you didn't use Hires root beer in a soda skeeting contest.

This was both a bitter and a sweet moment. Bitter because the boy cheated and we were soaked with soda. Everything we touched we stuck to it. We couldn't sit down on anything because we wouldn't be able to get unstuck. The sweet was that Cleo had finally broken into our ethical code of lying, cheating and stealing. We had some Toe Boys who could steal, some who lied, but now Cleo had two vices: he cheated, he lied about the soda he was using, and Frank said he was now a "calypso maniac." I think what Frank meant was he had become a kleptomaniac.

Man, when we got home every one of us got a whooping. It turned out that Cleo had broken into Doc's storage, and had stolen the sodas he distributed out to us. We didn't have any telephones, so I don't know how our parents got that information and conveyed it out so fast. So, we all went to bed with sore booties, and as I kneeled beside my bed that night, I prayed that Cleo's booty would be sorer than everybody's.

Uncle Buddy told me that we young folk were always letting "our head write a check that our booty would have to cash." I never did understand what he meant at the time, but today I get it.

A few days later, after our butts healed, Cleo, Frank, Jerry and I went to town and we decided we were going to get some food and go to a movie. We figured we had about three dollars and this was enough to get us a large bag of fries, sodas, some bonbons, and each of us a couple ten-cent hot dogs, but we had to get one of us in as a child. Children under a certain age were free, so we figured Jerry was the one to qualify. This boy was like a midget and was three years younger than we were and was small for his age. So we told Jerry he had to give the lady a date of birth that would make him a couple years younger than his actual age. When we got up to the booth where the ticket lady was, we gave her our money and told her that Jerry was only a child so he should get in free. She got off her stool and looked through the little round hole in the ticket booth just to see the top of Jerry's head.

She said to Jerry in a baby talk, "Oh, you have the little bitty one with you today, oh, he is so cute. Little one, how old are you?"

Now this a big mistake, because this boy's memory was about as long as his thing. Now we are thinking, we really got this broad, and we started singing, "Go Jerry, go Jerry, go Jerry go!"

Then Jerry told the girl he was born in a year that made him twenty-eight years old. She then told him, "Wow, you are older than I thought! You are twenty-eight years old. You must be a midget."

Now, I know this girl knew the boy wasn't that old, but because we were trying to get over on her, she charged him the full price. We are now at a high degree of pisstivity, because we now had to include another ticket in our budget. We went down to the hot dog stand, because hamburgers and bonbons were now out of the question. Pats and Arts sold fries in a box, and fifty cents could buy you enough fries that you had to carry them on your shoulder like a cotton sack.

We went to the movie, but no one wanted to sit with Jerry because he had cost us an extra quarter. I could only shun him for so long before I started feeling sorry for him. I knew he wanted to be next to me so I sat next to him, and he was asleep and leaning on me almost before the movie started.

Frank and Cleo looked at Jerry and said, “That little Negro cost us extra money, now he has the nerve to go to sleep on your arm?”

I guess Jerry always knew he was safe with me so I let him sleep in peace.

We rode back in a truck called the Gray Stallion, driven by Paul. This meant that Jerry was going to be attached to me somehow. He was always holding my hand, hanging on to my arm or sleeping in my lap. It really bugged me that he was always hanging on to me, but I loved him.

As soon as we got in the truck he wanted to sit in my lap. I knew he wanted to go to sleep, and I was tired of holding this little chocolate child. While traveling home, this horrific smell kept ascending into our nostrils. We knew somebody was farting and it was killing us. DJ was not there and this was DJ type gas. Jerry was on my lap and every time he would rise up this smell would emanate upward. I finally figured out it was Jerry. So every time he tried to lift up I would push his head down, because if you can’t lift up, you can’t have gas. That is simple logic. We all took turns holding his head down until we got to the house.

I loved little Jerry. One day we were in their living room, and I was tickling Jerry, and he was laughing out of control. I thought this was great. I got the little rascal going, and I made him laugh until it hurt. He got to a point where he couldn’t even breathe, and then the rascal peed in his britches. I then realized the boy almost died from laughter. I figured I’d better not tickle him again, because he could possibly defecate on himself, if I wasn’t careful.

It was a few days later that Jerry had a puppy that died and he wanted me to do the funeral. I did the funeral for the puppy and preached the eulogy, but that was just the beginning. He also had a rooster that died, and many of us were glad because we didn’t like that rooster in the first place.

He was always trying to peck people and would strut around like he owned the yard. Many nights I had dreamed of him on my plate covered in gravy and onions, with a couple of buttermilk biscuits and a big glass of Kool-Aid.

I didn't know why I let this boy hang around me. He always had me doing crazy things to keep him happy. He was much younger than me. He was like a tick that caused you to itch, and I was his host, and you had to scratch him to feel good.

His request that day was that I do a funeral for his rooster. Why me? I didn't even like going to church, but he cried so hard it gave him the hiccups. I certainly didn't like funerals. I still hadn't gotten over the puppy's funeral. I didn't like the rooster, but if I didn't do something Jerry was gonna start crying.

I couldn't take watching that little nappy head rascal cry, because when he cried, and the tears ran down his face, he looked like a chocolate bar melting. So I agreed to perform the funeral and eulogized this dumb hostile chicken. We went to the back of the house and dug a hole in the ground. The rooster wasn't even present because they had already eaten him, so we placed a rock in the hole in place of the rooster and covered it with dirt. Jerry made a cross from two ice cream sticks and placed it on the grave. He told me that I was supposed to give the rooster, who was already dead and eaten, his last rites. I'm thinking, *It's a little late for that.*

I told him, "I don't mind saying a few words, but I am not going to preach no sermon over some dead bird that you've already eaten."

Sure enough, the boy started crying, and I had to do the funeral and preach the sermon. Now, I'm thinking to myself, *What can I say that is good about this no-good, jumping-on-your-back, hostile, cowardly and ugly chicken, which will soon be defecation in the outhouse?* I really was happy to know he was dead. If this rooster would not have died when he did, I had plans of killing him myself. Of course, I would have to get in line behind Frank. I just wanted him dead for his covert attacks when I wasn't looking. Frank, well, I think Frank got hungry every time he looked at that rooster and that's why he wanted to ring his neck.

That rooster wasn't like other animals. He would never attack you face to face, but he waited until your back was turned, then he would attack you. He was really "chicken"!

The subject of my sermon, for the benefit of Jerry, of course, was "I done lost a friend, because the rooster done gone." Man, when I got to preaching, I put everything it. I almost preached that rooster back to life. I preached so hard I scared myself.

I was preaching, "Ooh Lord, I done lost a friend today, 'cause the rooster, I say the rooster done gone. One of these days, I will see this rooster up in chicken heaven. He won't have to worry about gravy or mashed potatoes being poured on him, because he will be where all good chickens go. He will be in chicken heaven. Oooohh Lord, we done lost a friend, 'cause the rooster done gone."

Jerry started singing, "This little light of mine, I'm gonna let it shine; let it shine, let it shine, let it shine."

As Jerry, Cleo and the others were singing, I thought, *This sucker ain't ever going to see chicken heaven, but if there is a hell for chickens, he's there sitting on a stump trying to figure out a way to jump on the devil's back, and raise more hell in hell.*

He would always jump on me when I wasn't looking and peck me on the butt. I said many times, "One of these days I'm going to bite you back and enjoy it." I regretted missing the opportunity of eating that bird, but I was glad he had gone to the hereafter.

Jerry started crying so hard he got the hiccups. Man, it really got to me. How could he have such feelings for this bird? I know I will never forget the funeral of that rooster or the puppy. Little did I know, that one day I would be preaching the gospel and doing funerals for the very people I love.

The next two days it rained so hard that it washed away our sorrows and there were no more lamentations for the rooster. It was time to move on with life. It was time to go hunting to forget the sad events. We went out into the desert down by the river and found a hole that was full of rainwater and ducks were swimming around as if they were just waiting for us.

Morris, Frank, DJ, Lee, myself and others were looking at these ducks and all we could think about was dinnertime. Going through our heads were all the ways we could have these ducks on a plate. Duck with biscuits and gravy, duck with welfare cheese, duck with welfare rice, duck with brother rabbit syrup, and duck with corn flakes.

We started sneaking up on those ducks, step by step, inch by inch, then we started crawling slowly on our bellies and getting closer and closer. A couple of them flew away. As they flew into the horizon, it felt like having your plate filled with food and then dropping it on the ground.

I signaled the brothers to stop, because it seemed that we were getting awful close. The ducks that remained just kept floating around and not paying us any attention. Now by that time, I'm rather offended that they took us so lightly. I gave the signal to blow them out of the water. Man, we had .22-caliber rifles, BB guns, and a shotgun. So we unloaded. *Ping! Bang! Boom! Boom! Ping! Bang! Boooom!* Bullets were hitting all around those ducks and they kept swimming.

I re-evaluated the situation and suggested that we get closer because they were probably deaf ducks. We got closer and opened up again with everything we had. When we stopped shooting, the waterline around the pond had dropped about a foot, because we probably knocked a foot of water out of it.

Now, a normal person would have realized long time ago that there was something wrong with those ducks, but we were so excited we couldn't think straight. Man, we had time to reload and shoot again. We were knocking their heads off; their wings were floating around in the water. It was strange, because we would shoot their heads off, but they would still be floating upright without their heads. Suddenly we heard someone yelling.

This White man came over to the pond screaming at us, "You boys get away from that pond; you boys done destroyed all my decoys! Darn nit, don't y'all know decoys when ya see them? Get the hell away from that pond!"

Man, we took off running scared, but curious, because we never heard of any ducks called decoys. Frank wanted to go back, because he said a decoy was the name of a certain kind of duck, like the mallard or blue gross. It took a while before I learned from Uncle Buddy that we had shot a piece of wood. Frank was upset, because he said we should have brought one home and cooked it, just to see if it was real. I know we left an impression on the guy who owned the decoys. After all, they did lose their heads over us and some didn't have a leg to stand on.

School ended for the year and we had to go chop cotton to get money.

We went to work for this half-breed name Tomas. He was a brother that was half-Mexican. Tomas would sell us burritos, tacos and tamales, and by the end of the week, some of us were lucky if we didn't end up owing Tomas most of our money. Anything other than biscuits and Spam, potted meat and crackers, was a welcome treat. It took a great deal of temperance just to come out of them fields with a few dollars.

One day during lunchtime Frank went to sleep, which was common to do. Frank was lying on his back with his arms folded across his chest like you do when you're lying in a coffin. He had a nightmare in the daytime and was grunting and rocking from side to side. Finally he just disappeared. When we went to the spot where he was, we realized he had rolled down the hill while he was having a "daymare."

I yelled to Cleo, "Look at Frank rolling down the hill!"

We looked in amazement then we started singing, "Go Frank go!"

The boy got up angry and threatening to kill us because we didn't wake him up. Frank told us that he had gone over to the other side, but we told him all he had done was hit his big head against a couple of rocks that were now broken.

"You must have a concussion," I said.

"My head is not a cushion," Frank responded.

At that point I refused to try and explain to Frank the difference between a concussion and a cushion. You have to understand that we are not dealing with a rocket scientist here or with anyone who has an extensive vocabulary. Boys like Frank, Lee, DJ and Leroy are lucky they learned how to walk before they were ten. Well, except for Leroy, that boy probably ran out of his mother's womb with a basketball and a football in his hands.

I loved them Toe Boys, and it wasn't for their minds. I think some of them had lost their minds long before we met. I loved them, and we all loved growing up in the Toe.

Growing up in the Toe was not always funny. There were times when things were very serious. There were times when each of us at one time fell in love or had some serious feelings toward some girl. I mean when you care enough to buy them a MoonPie or let them drink out of the same R.C. bottle that you drank from, that is love.

Leroy claimed that I had lost my mind, because I actually shared a

MoonPie with a girl and admitted to letting her drink from my bottle of R.C. Cola. Leroy said my mind had warped, and I would never recover from such a meltdown. He told everyone that my condition was past the point of returning to sanity. He wasn't sure if I was stable enough to be the leader of the Nightriders. Can you imagine Leroy being a single person insurrection or a one-man coup?

This all started when I went to Avra Valley to visit my cousin Sonny, who we called Swank. We called him Swank because he thought he was God's gift to women. The only reason I liked that boy was because he was kinfolk and Mama told me I had to, and he had a lot of toys.

Avra Valley was like the suburb of the Toe. In fact, any town or city near the area of Rillito was the suburb of the Toe. It didn't matter how big the town or city, you have to understand that the Toe was the world to us. Like in the biblical times when people thought Egypt was the world, that is the way we felt about the Toe. Phoenix, Tucson and surrounding areas were a branch of Rillito.

CHAPTER NINE

Love at First Sight

I went to Swank's house and when I walked in the door I saw the most beautiful girl I had ever seen in my life. Now, I never thought, if this is his sister then she is my cousin. I had seen her at school many times, and I don't know why I never noticed her before. I remember one time the kids were putting chips on each other's shoulders and daring people to knock them off. Someone had put a chip on my shoulder and Jessie came up to knock it off, and I hit her in the stomach and made her cry. I thought she couldn't be the same person. Man, she had gotten beautiful. I thought maybe it was his adopted sister. I had seen Jessie many times, but this time she looked different. She blew me away with her looks, and I thought, *This boy ain't supposes to have someone looking that good in the same house with him.* I fell in love with Jessie and thank God she liked me too, I think.

When we first saw each other we just sat there staring at each other for five minutes. I thought, *She never looked like this before!* Her hair was long and beautiful, she had a light complexion (that meant something back then), and she smelled good. Most girls her age smelled like dirt and wanted to hit you all the time, but she had changed. I went and told the boys, this is it, I have found my thrill, and it wasn't on Blueberry Hill, but down in Avra Valley.

We went from elementary through junior high together and I decided there was no way I would ever flunk and pass up the opportunity of spending each grade with her. Man, when she passed, I passed. I was in love and we shared things together. She gave me cookies and some candy. All children know that is a strong indication of love.

One day at school during Christmas season, while in the third grade, she sang "Away in a Manger" and I cried like a baby. Everything about her was beautiful: her voice, her looks and the way she talked. After she finished singing we exchanged gifts, and she gave me a huge Hershey bar and a box of Fig Newton cookies. No one had ever given me something of such substance, heartfelt meaning and magnitude. Even the Toe Boys admitted, "This must be love." Girls just didn't give you a large Hershey bar unless they were head over heels in love. This was indeed proof that we had a never-ending love. This was something that could develop from Hershey bar to Hershey kisses.

I finally was able to get Leroy and the others to accept my situation. I told them that we had chemistry between us and there was warmth between us. Leroy then told the guys that it was now evident that I had truly lost my mind.

He said, "The boy done shared MoonPies, colas, Delaware Punch, Oreos and Fig Newtons with the girl. Now he comes here talking biology and chemistry, you know he is either crazy or insane."

We went together from the third grade through the fifth grade. The fifth grade was when my world crumbled before my eyes, my heart sank, and my dreams dissipated like steam from a kettle. Jessie, who was called Dixie by some relatives, was my first love, even though I didn't ever remember kissing her. To me, she was the most beautiful girl in school. I just knew that one day we would be married and all our children would be as beautiful as she was. I would name our girls Jessie one, Jessie two, Jessie three, all the way up to Jessie thirty. Then I would name the boys Codas one, Codas two, up to thirty as well. I had figured it all out. We would have sixty children!

Then one day they moved to the Toe next to us. I would go over and hold her hand. My heart would beat so fast I thought I could hear the sound through my shirt. I thought I would have a heart attack and die. I knew that a heart only had so many beats before it stopped, and I was afraid mine would be used up in one day. That's what it was like being next to her.

When I was in her presence, it was the only time I couldn't find anything to say.

One day I brought her home to my mom and that's when my mother truly broke my heart. She told me that we were close cousins and marriage was indeed out of the question. I begged and pleaded for us to be boyfriend and girlfriend for life and promised we wouldn't have children, but Mom said, "No!" I even promised if we were married, I would sleep in a different room, I would never kiss her, just hug her, but Mama laughed and said, "No way!"

Jessie and I couldn't be together, but I will love her always. I knew there would never be another, and I would have to live the rest of my life from the third grade on, never to love another. I was destined to live a life of celibacy forever. They call it puppy love, but no matter what people call it, it's still love. Love as a child is called puppy love, with me it had grown to be a big dog.

I must have cried for days, but I wouldn't let the Toe Boys see me. Even to this day when I see Jessie there is something very special about the way I feel about her. I will always care about her, because she was one of the first girls to care about me. She has always been a dear friend, because that is all we were allowed to be to each other. I knew that one day we would both be married to different people, but I would always have a place in my heart for Jessie no matter what the future would bring. I will always wonder what could have been if blood wasn't in the way. Perhaps one of us could have rescued the other from some disastrous relationship.

We went through junior high together, and she saw me play in my first basketball game. I remember the first basket I ever made in the sixth grade, even though it was in the wrong basket and was credited to the other team. Just the thought of her being there eased the pain.

About six months before we graduated from junior high, she had gotten pregnant by someone who was old enough to have been arrested for child molesting. She did graduate from junior high wearing a maternity dress. She exemplified a great deal of courage and I believe if things could have been different for her, the sky would have been the limit. She was a very smart person at her age, but apparently very innocent. I was really proud of her and put my arms around her that night to congratulate her; afterwards, I walked away with tears in my eyes. Those tears shed that night were tears she would never see. I could see the hopelessness that this had brought about, and that her fate had been sealed. I found me a quiet place, and as I cried, I prayed just for her.

Even now I wonder what her potential could have been. I will always love Jessie and have a platonic attachment for her and have a place in my heart for her. I believe in my heart that Jessie will always have a place for me. I knew that as we got older she would eventually get married and have children, but in retrospect I thank God for my first puppy love. I do wonder how her parents could allow someone much older to date her. Today this act of sexual involvement with a minor would have been considered a criminal offense, and the suspect would have been arrested. The irony of this was that he was a police officer.

Life continued on and I continued with it. Man, them boys in the Toe was so bad that in order to be safe, I would go to the post office and see if any of them had their picture on the wall. If their picture weren't in the post office, then I would relax. No matter how much Cleo stole, Frank attempted to fight everyone, or DJ prophesied about the future, they were never on the wall. A couple of times I had a scare, because I thought I saw Frank and Syl. I could never figure it out, because I knew for a fact Frank should have been on the list several times. Gootee definitely should have been on the posters; in fact, I thought about turning Gootee in myself.

I thought the letters FBI stood for the Frightened, Black and the Ignorant. It seemed that everybody on the posters were Black; even the White folk looked Black. They all looked like someone took their picture right after they woke up from a nightmare, and they all looked familiar.

I heard you could justify criminal behavior by saying that the suspects usually came from a broken home. That was ridiculous because everybody in the Toe came from a broken home. There was something broken in everybody's house: a window, a door, a bed, a couch, the ceiling, the roof or a chair or something. Half the time our parents were broke: I mean they were flat broke!

They also said that folk got involved in crime because they were poor. Some people in the Toe were so poor they couldn't pay their bills, but we were so poor that we couldn't even pay attention. If you could be arrested for being poor then the whole community should have been in prison.

Well, the time had come for another contest. We called this the pooting (passing gas) contest of '59. Frankie (Tater), Bernie's son, was there. He was as thin as the cutting edge of a Gillette razorblade. You could shave with him.

DJ was there and he was so weird. There were rumors that he had been taken up by aliens, but I heard after the anal probe, the aliens had rejected him. It had been reported that because of DJ being rejected by the aliens, none of the residents of the Toe would receive further consideration.

We decided to let DJ be the judge. DJ said the elements of a good poot were its duration, how bad it smelled and the sound. Some of the guys didn't have a chance because they ate good food. We thought eating good food took away the odiferous smell. If you ate good food you could have the sound and duration, but the smell would never be gross enough.

We allowed everyone to participate, because there was no entry fee, but you had to be a Toe Boy. Lee was first and did well for his size, but though it lasted three seconds, it didn't have a bad smell. In fact, after Lee pooted, everybody got hungry. Paul was next, and he was known as one of the best. He always had endurance and the unusual thing about Paul's poots was that though most people pooted in base, Paul did it in tenor. Paul went for five seconds, but his mistake was he had gotten up early that morning and made him some Toe cereal. Toe cereal is unsalted crackers with milk and sugar. Because he had a decent breakfast there was no bad stench.

Cleo was next and this boy just sat there straining, but couldn't pass gas. We moved him off the "poot stand" and went to the next contestant. Jerry, of course, was a natural gasser, but he laughed all the time he pooted. Jerry's poot had a bad smell, but no duration because his laughter accelerated the poot and created intermittent sounds.

Yours truly was next and though I'd had a good breakfast of brother rabbit syrup and butter, biscuits and a couple of bacon strips, I did reasonably well. DJ told us he heard a scream coming from the planter before the roses withered and collapsed. This put me in first place and the prize was a strawberry popsicle. We had each put in a penny and it cost six cents.

I was about to receive my honors when DJ, who was the judge, decided he wanted to participate. Now that's like a sports official, stopping the game so he can play. He would always come late for everything and be the last one to enter. You had to let him in because he would tell the world if you didn't. DJ was good at these kinds of things because he always practiced. He was also the best poot judge in Arizona and surrounding states. He could listen to a poot then smell it and tell you what you had eaten. There are wine connoisseurs, but DJ was a fart connoisseur.

Folk would poot and DJ would listen, smack his lips like he tasted the air, take a deep breath, and begin to tell you what you had for lunch. He would say after someone pooted; you ate two helpings of black-eyed peas, corn on the cob, one pig feet and you drank Kool-Aid from a mayonnaise jar. The boy was good!

A few days earlier Jerry and I were in the house and I had a half a bottle of Pepsi cola that I set on the piano. When I got back, it was gone, but Jerry swore that he didn't do it. He lied and said he was just eating some fried potatoes. While we were sitting around wondering who did it, DJ came by. Jerry made a serious mistake when he pooted, but no one could hear it.

DJ yelled out, "Wow, somebody did a 'silencer' and whoever did it had fried potatoes and a half a bottle of Pepsi." Then he said, "The Pepsi didn't even belong to the man who pooted."

Everybody turned and said in unison, "JERRY!"

Now you know that's good. We knew DJ was talented and watched him sit there swallowing air and preparing himself. When DJ pooted, the house trembled, the wallpaper came off one side of the wall, roofing nails popped out of the roof, and a sheet of sheetrock that was leaning against the house outside felled down. Then we heard this noise coming from outside and it was the dogs howling in the Toe. We ran from the house to get air and away from the smell. It was too little too late, because the smell had penetrated our garments. The dogs jumped on us and started licking our clothes.

We were so impressed that we gave DJ the popsicle. We started playing in the yard and it seemed that the smell of DJ's fart just wouldn't go away. We started thinking nobody's fart should last that long, so we made DJ pull down his pants and we checked his Fruit of the Loom. Sure enough, the boy had signs of do-do on his Fruit of the Loom, so we had to disqualify him. One of the rules was that you were not allowed to do-do (defecate) during the poot.

He claimed it was an old stain and asked if we wanted to check by touching it. Now DJ had a point, but no one was going to touch his underwear. It was known that DJ wore underwear for two to three weeks at a time. If someone did chisel the stain, a piece of it could chip off and hit you up side the head and put you in a coma. Since no one would check we allowed him to have the popsicle and to be the official winner of the contest.

Once I saw his grandmother washing his underwear, and after she let them soak for a day or two, she would beat them with a Roger Morris baseball bat.

A few days later we met at my house and played night basketball at the handmade court. We had nailed a small bicycle rim to the back of a three-feet-square piece of plywood and nailed that to a wooden pole sticking out of the ground about ten feet tall. Our net was a croaker sack tied to the rim and hanging down so it would slow the ball down when it went through. Sometimes we would tie the end so the ball would stay in the basket when it went in, and we wouldn't have to go chasing it down the dirt road. We later decided not to tie the end of the net, because it eliminated the fast break.

The game started at nine p.m. so we had to get two old car tires and put them at each end of the court and set them on fire. That was our light, and when that burnt low sometimes we would designate someone to stand at the basket and shine a lantern toward the basket. This had to be an honest person, so it was always difficult to find a person who wasn't partial to one team or the other. We had to totally rely on this person's honesty and integrity. I mean, when you're doing a fade-away jumper, twenty feet away, the only way you would know if you hit it or not would be if the designator shouted, "Count it!"

Now, we didn't have any impartial folk among us. Frank and Leroy would lie and say they didn't have any parents just to get a free lunch at the school. Clevie Lee, a.k.a. Sheep, was my cousin and Leroy's nephew. Frank and Sheep would tell us to flip a coin for shirts and skins. Everybody knew you couldn't be shirts or skins at night. We all knew that the skins had an advantage, because you couldn't see them boys in the dark.

The rim started coming loose so we held DJ on our shoulders, and he nailed the rim back on. The game was on, and Leroy went up in the air during the game and shot a jumper, but the ball stuck inside the rim. In a professional game the ball sticks on the outside of the rim. We couldn't figure out why the ball stuck in the inside of the rim. When we got it off the rim the air started slowly coming out. Then, yours truly hit a five-foot jumper and again the ball stuck. Now I'm thinking this is ridiculous, so we called time-out to investigate the matter. We borrowed some matches from Syl, because he smoked and always had matches on him. We lit the match and held Frank on our shoulders to see what was wrong. We probably would have gotten higher if we just jumped, because Frank was so short. When Frank put the lit match near the rim we could all see that DJ had nailed the nails in facing the court and didn't bend them down. They were puncturing the ball every time we took a shot.

We borrowed some electrical tape and taped the ball and bent the nails down so we could continue playing. We didn't have an air pump so we had to get someone who could blow air into a ball. So we called on Syl, and he blew air right through the little hole until the ball was tight. Sometimes we would have to let some air out so the ball wouldn't burst.

The ball kept losing its air, and we were frustrated until DJ came up with one of his brilliant ideas. He said, "Instead of dribbling, just pretend to dribble by pumping your arms in a downward motion."

This was working okay until Frank and Sheep would get the ball and pump their arms twice between one end of the court to the other, and swear they didn't travel. It was evident that some of the guys could not be trusted with the pretend dribble. They would lie to their mama and daddy, and there was no way I was going to trust them with the pretend dribble.

We changed the rule and said when you got the ball, you had to pass it, but you were allowed two steps if you were going to do a layup and one step for a jump shot.

Night after night we would play in the dark, and it got to a point where the only person who could shoot in the dark was Leroy. Sometimes we would have a volunteer stand next to the basket with a "may shine flashlight." That was a flashlight that may or may not shine, it all depended on how the flashlight felt. You had to shake it up to wake it up, so it would shine.

The rest of us would shoot and the spotter was always saying, "miss, miss" but whenever Leroy shot, he would say, "two" or "three," if it were a three-pointer. Of course we had instituted this stupid rule that DJ had thought of called "the three-point shot." This was 1959, whoever heard of a three-point shot? Man, the only place in the world that had a three-point shot was the Toe in1959.

DJ said somewhere in the future they would add the three-point shot if you made the shot from a certain distance away from the basket. He said in the years to come they would have another range, and it would be the four-point shot. Again, we told him how stupid his idea was and that this would never be instituted, at least not in the United States.

It seemed that whenever Leroy took a shot it sounded like a stuck record: two, two, three and three! I could not believe Leroy could be making everything he was throwing up, so I volunteered to be the spotter. Sure enough, this boy was being knocked around, bumped out of bounds and sometimes three players would be all over him, and he would still make it. Sometimes I would say, "miss" just so the boy would seem human.

Then Leroy would say, "Are you sure, Codas? That felt like it went in." He would then take the ball and duplicate his previous shot. He would say, "You see, Codas, I took the ball like this, then I went to my left, then went up like this and shot the ball."

The ball would go in again just like it did the first time.

Then he would say, "That felt good, now did that one go in?"

"Yeah, that went in, but the first one didn't," I said, of course with my fingers crossed.

The others would get frustrated and urge us to go on with the game. Leroy would shoot the ball and turn around and start going towards the other basket. He would then turn around with his hand in the air making a gesture of a ball going through the net and say with perfect timing "two" just as the ball went *shwish* through the sack we used for a net.

I believe God gave Leroy talent to make up for what was missing upstairs. I think the reason we loved him so much was because Leroy was ignorant of his greatness and sometimes it reflected in humbleness. I never heard Leroy brag about his talents, but he would challenge you at the drop of hat, like all the Toe Boys would.

Whenever we had games in the Toe, we had to divide the teams a certain way to prevent certain people from being on the same team. Frank and Sonny (Swank) could never be on the same team, because they were always refereeing the games while they played. They both lied about every call so we divided them up so we wouldn't have the two referees on the same team. Swank was my cousin and so was Sheep. Sheep was kind of extraordinarily dark, and that was a benefit when we played at night. He was short and stocky. I guess the best way to describe him would be in the words of an old Black man named Cadillac who once said, "That boy is damn near a midget."

Clevie Lee (Sheep) became my nighttime weapon. I would tell him to break for a pass and just when he decided to cut for the ball, he was to clap his hands when he was open. Every time the boy did this he would be open and I would get the ball to him. Unfortunately he couldn't catch, so half the times he would turn the ball over. It didn't matter how many times Clevie Lee would break open, or how hard we tried, Leroy was killing us. Man, we couldn't even lie the ball out of the basket, because Leroy would get the ball and show us how he did the shot and the ball would go in just like it did the first time.

I figured the only way to stop him was to bulldog him. I intended on burying my elbow deep into his chest to slow him down. He got the ball and went up for a jump shot. Now, I couldn't jump with this boy, so I went as high as I could, in an attempt to elbow him in the chest, and ended up hitting him on his thigh. This was the only boy in the world who shot a jump shot downward. We had a tire burning that also gave us warmth and light, and Leroy landed in the fire from the push I gave him and stepped out of the burning fire like nothing was wrong. Leroy was hotter than the fire and didn't feel a thing!

We noticed before he shot the free throw that his tennis shoes were smoking. It wasn't bothering us that they were ahead by thirty points, because everyone knows that at the end of the game someone always yells out, "the next two out of three wins!"

We were playing "make it take it." If you made it, you took it out of bounds, and you maintained possession. They let us have the ball first thinking we didn't have a chance. The first thing I did was to tell Clevie Lee to get under the basket and move around.

"Don't grin and don't open your eyes," I whispered, "until I call your name, then clap your hands, so I can throw the ball in the direction of the sound."

Now, I didn't mean for him to literally close his eyes, but he took me serious, but I did mean for him not to grin.

He took off with his eyes closed and was bumping into everybody. No one could see him at night and it was like bumping into the invisible man. You knew he was there, but you couldn't see him. I figured he ought to be there by now so I yelled, "Sheep!" He was Black and was treated like an outcast so we called him sheep with the word Black understood as a prefix (Black Sheep). He clapped his hands when he thought he was open, and I got the ball to him, and he banked it in. At this point you only counted a point a basket. We were up by one and still had the ball.

We tried the same play again, but this time Cleo figured it out and was feeling around near the basket and felt Sheep's presence, so when I threw the ball, Cleo stole it. Cleo passed the ball to Leroy, and we knew he was going to score. I went up with him and I'm looking at his waistband, and we are both at our peak.

He was about to hit his famous jumper when I yelled, "Leroy, your shoe is on fire!"

Leroy had been scared of fire since he fell on the fire over at the cottonwood tree near the ditch. He screamed and turned the ball loose and grabbed his foot. I got the ball out of the air and shot it. The ball banked off the board and went in for the win. My teammates were jumping up and down, high-fiving each other, but me, I'm on the ground looking up at Leroy wondering, *How long can he hang in the air like that?*

He finally come down on top of me and then started running towards his house. We knew he was going to tell his mama we had set him on fire again, so DJ stomped the fire out with his barefoot, and we all ran to our houses.

The next day Leroy's mama, Mrs. Tiny, came to the house, and I knew I was going to get a whooping. She told Mama that Leroy said he got his foot burned accidentally. He didn't blame us for trying to burn him up like last time. She just didn't want us to hurt "her little sweet baby."

Now, the only thing sweet on Leroy was his tooth. He could eat a box of chocolates, two big hunks and a big-time candy bar without blinking an eye. I think that's where he got all that energy. I told the others that it was safe for them to come out of their houses, because we weren't going to get a whooping. Leroy hadn't blamed us for his foot burning.

Most of the boys in the Toe had to chop cotton in the summertime and pick cotton in the wintertime. They paid us three dollars per hundred pounds of cotton when we picked it and paid us five dollars a day when we chopped it.

During the summer we would see literally thousands of grasshoppers in the fields. Whenever we got close to one we would hold the hoe as if it was a spear or plunger (of course, we had never seen a plunger, because outhouses didn't have flushing toilets). We would get close to a grasshopper that had landed on our row, and as we poised to smash him with the back of the hoe, we would call out loud an amount: "Penny or nickel, sometimes even a dime."

If someone yelled out an amount or said "gotcha," then the bet was covered. If you killed the grasshopper, you won the bet, and of course, if you didn't, you lost. By the end of the day it was all or nothing and we would always end up even.

If you had to urinate, you just found you a bush and took care of business, but if you had to defecate you had to make sure there was no snake in the bushes. You had to take a piece of newspaper, magazine paper, a stick or a leaf of some kind to clean yourself. By the end of the day there were a lot of people walking really weird. Many people came out of them fields walking like they had been on a horse all day. That is why we all went to the irrigation ditch to bathe after work.

Chopping and picking cotton was fun except the times when Gootee would eat everybody's lunch or put a dead snake on one of the girl's rows. It was during those times that the boys started to notice some of the girls like Earley, Joyce, Lena and others.

Joyce was Frank's sister, and we called her Lady. Joyce was always like a sister to me, and I cared for her as such. There was a time or two when a spark would fly between us, but it never caused a fire.

Now the other girl's name was Earley and because of that I decided to be different and called her Late.

You could tell the boys were noticing, because all the girls had to do was get a row next to one of us and walk with a hoe in their hands. We would chop all the weeds on their row. It was as if those girls had grown up overnight. It seemed that their breasts developed overnight, and they all started looking like real girls. Their hands got soft, their smiles got prettier, they smelled nicer, and their shape changed astoundingly.

One day you're looking at an ugly caterpillar, and then the next day it's a beautiful butterfly. I never really considered them as ugly caterpillars, but the metamorphosis seemed to take place overnight.

I remember a girl named Jean. She was also called Marcie. We were about the same age, maybe she was a couple of years older, but girls seem to mature a lot sooner than boys. I would pick sugar cane from the fields and bring her the best stalks. She played me like a pickup game on the basketball court. She was dating a guy in town who had a beautiful '57 Chevy and all I had was a put-together bicycle that wasn't working. I had about as much of a chance of dating her as I did changing my race.

I believe that life is a wheel and what goes around will come around. I knew that one day she would have to reap what she sowed. I liked her a lot, and I treated her like a lady in my own childish way until she disappeared from the Toe. Of course, that happened quite a bit. One day they're there and then they meet someone from town, and then they would disappear. It was a phenomenon that occurred often in the Toe with the girls.

I began to wonder if I would ever leave the Toe and what it would take to get me away from the place I loved. I was watching our boss who was an Oriental man. He came to the cotton field driving a brand new vehicle. I was attending school with his kids and had known them for a long time.

As I stood there gazing at the vehicle and daydreaming, old Cadillac walked up to me and said, "I know what ya thinking, boy, but the only way ya can get to where he is, is by getting an education."

For a moment, all I could think was, *There has to be a better way.* It was then that I truly begin to think, maybe Cadillac was right, an education was the vehicle to prosperity and deliverance.

CHAPTER TEN

The Storm

There were always storms, both natural and spiritual, coming through the Toe, but we always managed to survive. There were times when it was very frightening, but somehow we prayed our way through.

My father was born in 1896 and was a veteran of World War 1. Somewhere along life's journey he learned to do many things. He was a good farmhand and could do ranch work as well. He didn't spend much time in the fields before he was hired to work at a place called El Rancho Grande.

Soon afterwards, my father purchased three cabins and an acre of land in the Toe. The three cabins faced each other in the form of a triangle. One was used for a kitchen, and the other two were bedrooms. We had an icebox that stood in the patio, which was the dirt area between the cabins. There was no electricity at first and no running water. We had wood heaters and wood stoves. We purchased our ice from thc icc man, and it was kept in an icebox.

My father started building a brick house and before it was completed we decided to move in and finish it as we went. The rooms were petitioned with sheetrock, but you could look up and see the roof through an open ceiling. The cabins were still there and Mom would cook her meals in the kitchen cabin. The other bedroom cabins remained accessible, and sometimes when my buddies came over we would sleep in them. The rest of the family would sleep in the unfinished house.

We were glad for the move and very proud that we actually had a house to live in. The house that Daddy built was only a few feet away from the cabins we lived in initially.

One day we had company visiting us from Continental, and my nephew Billy was visiting from town as well. We were all playing in the neighborhood when some very strange, stormy-looking clouds appeared. My father and the other adults in the Toe were very apprehensive about the situation. Dad called me home, and we started boarding up the windows and doors. Suddenly it got dark and the wind became violent. Everyone was in the big house when the storm hit.

Billy was visiting for the summer, and he was a year or two younger than me. He and I decided to go to the cabin to get my favorite dish, red chili beans. My mom could cook the best beans in the world. She would put chili and chorizo in them, and you never knew what kind of meat she would add. Sometimes it was ground beef, sometimes pigskins, pigtails, pig feet or ox tails. The meat was always a surprise.

Well, there was no storm big enough to keep me away from Mama's chili beans. So Billy and I sneaked out the back door and headed for the cabin where the beans were. The wind was so ferocious we could see the cabin was about to blow over. The dust inside the cabin was swirling and blinding. We could hardly see each other. I figured the beans would be okay if I kept them covered. The cabin rose off the ground and then landed back in place, as if some giant had picked it up to peek and see if we were there, then dropped it.

I told Billy, "It's time to get out of here!"

That fool had to have another scoop. That scoop almost cost us our lives. Just as Billy took that last scoop, the cabin blew off the foundation, and we both fell to the ground on our stomachs. We were crawling on our bellies, holding up the bowl of beans like a soldier would hold up his rifle. We saw and heard strange sounds as things blew over us, and debris from houses barely missed us as we crawled along the ground. Hogs were being rolled on the ground like tires, and roofs were being torn off houses. There were tree branches flying through the air and cars were rolling along without drivers. The force of the wind was so great that Billy and I were being rolled over, yet we continued to hold the bowl of beans in an upright position. Our instinct told us not to stand or we would blow away like paper. Twice we were rolled against Mama's chicken coop, and it kept us from being blown into the next county. I was leading Billy and we crawled fifty feet on the ground and finally made it to the back door. At this point we couldn't see a thing, and I questioned if Billy was still there with me.

I turned and shouted, "Billy!"

He responded, "I'm here, I'm here!"

I wondered if those inside realized that we were gone and would they hear our feeble knock? We tried with all our strength, but there was no response. We were holding on for dear life to the cement step in front of the door. I prayed, *Please God not like this.* I didn't want my life to be lost over a bowl of beans. Billy was holding onto my legs with both hands, he had decided to let the beans go and live. I held my bowl with one hand and was determined not to let go. I figured if we made it, I would have those beans, and it would not have been in vain. I was about to turn loose the bowl when I heard the sound of unlatching, and the door slowly opened. It was Dad and his friend fighting against the wind and trying to give us the space we needed to crawl through. Dad reached and grabbed my arm and started dragging me while his friend held the door firmly. As Dad pulled me in, along came Billy still wrapped around my legs like electrical tape.

Dad said, "Go to your mom's bedroom, quickly!"

My parents' bedroom was in the center of the house and had the strongest supports.

I was thanking God for my deliverance when I remembered my beans. I looked into the bowl and could see nothing but a bowl of mud. I thought to myself, *I could have died for this?*

The storm was not over, and as I entered the room, Mama and Mrs. Mosely, a visitor from Continental, were on their knees praying. My dad and Mr. Mosely were not believers, and they were just sitting there shaking and hoping the women were getting through. A strange thing happened, the wind took even a more violent turn, and as we looked up we could see the roof starting to rise off the studs that held it down. The studs could not hold it any longer, and the roof lifted up from the walls and was suspended in that position. The rain was pouring in and you could see the dark stormy sky through the opening. It was then that I realized that God is an on-time God.

My sister Mary began to shout as the Spirit of God came upon her. She started speaking in tongues, and she turned and faced that uplifted roof that was hanging in suspension. The wind was blowing her hair, and the rain was in her face, but she stood her ground. She began to talk to it in an unknown tongue. She pointed to it and commanded it to stop and return to its rightful position. I didn't understand the language she spoke, but in my spirit I knew what was said. I was able to interpret her words.

Again she spoke, "In the name of Jesus, I command you to stop rising and return to your rightful position!"

The wind ceased immediately and the roof returned to its position and fastened itself to the walls. It was as though she had commanded the elements by the power and authority of Almighty God. My dad and his friend were in awe of what they had witnessed, but Mama and her friend never looked up; they just kept praying.

I was reminded of the story in the Bible when Joshua fought against the Amorites. He said in the sight of Israel, "*Sun, stand thou still upon Gibeon and thou moon, in the valley of Ajalon. And the sun stood still and the moon stayed until the people had avenged themselves upon their enemies...*" (Joshua 10:12-13, KJV).

I loved my mother and Mrs. Mosely, but it was my sister Mary who I wanted to be close to at that moment. I watched God work in her that night and my faith increased a hundredfold. From that moment we could hear the wind blowing, but our home seemed to be in the eye of the storm. There was silence all around us, and you could hear everyone praying and thanking God for our deliverance. Even Dad and Mr. Mosely said, "Well, thank the Lord!"

When the storm was finally over we assessed the damage. Several homes had their roofs torn off. Lee and Duck's house was one of them. They had a storm cellar and had found shelter in it until the storm was over. Thank God they were okay. I can never forget the picture in my mind of Duck's mother standing in her kitchen the next day without a roof. God had spared their lives, and she acknowledged that fact. She looked like she was a full-blooded Indian, and she lifted up Christ as she talked boldly to me about the storm.

Water had come into all the houses because they were so poorly made. The cabin that Billy and I had entered had blown over. Electrical lines were down and there were dead animals all over the place. Mr. Mosely's car had been pushed about three hundred feet from where it was parked, but it seemed to be okay. They were able to drive home to Continental. We later heard sirens along the freeway tending to a motorist. Apparently a truck driver's semi-truck had blown over and he was killed.

We took inventory of the people and, thanks be to God, we were all alive. I noticed that no relief came to the Toe. No authorities came to see if anyone needed help. There were no White folk who were concerned enough to come from town and see about our little community of Black people. No sheriff deputy or rescue workers drove by out of concern or curiosity. We all came together to help those who suffered severely and we were not concerned about who didn't try to help us after the storm. Our help came through the storm. Almost every home in the Toe had someone inside who believed in God, and those who didn't, vicarious faith covered them as well. As it is written, "*I will lift mine eyes unto the hills from which cometh my help; my help cometh from the Lord, which made the heaven and earth*" (Psalms 121:1-2, KJV).

I became a witness that day to the awesome power of prayer. It reminded me of the time when Christ was in the ship and was awaken by the disciples asking for help. The Bible said, "*...He arose, and rebuked the wind, and said unto the sea, Peace, be still and the wind ceased, and there was a great calm*" (Mark 6:53, KJV). We didn't have to depend on the might of agencies or the power of the system, but as it is written, "*...not by might nor by power, but by my Spirit, saith the Lord*" (Zechariah 4:6, KJV).

We made it through that storm and many others. God brought us through both natural storms and the storms of life. We never looked behind us, but always looked forward, wondering what the new day would bring. As we grew up in the Toe, it was inevitable that just like the seasons, puberty would be on schedule. We were getting to that point in life when we started seeing girls differently than before.

I started liking Lena along with half of the Toe and the city of Tucson. I think when someone has that kind of attention it has to affect their mind. The boys in the Toe could not compete with the guys in town. We were riding bicycles, and they were driving cars. We were offering the girls sodas and candy bars, but the guys in the city were buying them dresses and shoes. I thought those were things you bought your wife when you got married, not your girlfriend.

It seemed like every time I tried to show Lena that I cared, she would throw up some barrier to denigrate me. I hadn't felt this way about a person since Jessie. I did fall in love with Lena, but I must admit when compared to what I felt for Jessie, there was something missing. I guess it was because in this case I gave love out, but love never returned. She seemed to like whoever gave her the most, so we couldn't compete with the older guys, because they had so much more to give.

I learned at an early age that there is a difference between love and lust. When you love someone, you love the whole person, what's on the inside and what is on the outside. When you lust after someone, it's all about the outside, and not what's on the inside. I think in my case this was a one-sided love affair, and it was my side doing the loving, and her side involved in the affair. I guess since we never made any commitment to each other, and I doubt if she even knew what I felt; with that in mind, she had the right to like whomever she wanted.

I remember going to her house one Christmas Eve with a Christmas gift. I had a beautiful jewelry box with mirrors, and it played a song whenever it was opened. I bought it at McClellan's and it cost me two days' wages. I had been from store to store in town, and had shopped in the rain and the cold to try and get her something to let her know how I felt. When I got to Lena's house there were so many gifts from so many people placed around the tree. The boys from the city were sitting around on the couch staring at each other. I was almost embarrassed to give her mine. After a short prayer and holy boldness, I gave the gift to her mother, because Lena was in another room. Her mother sensed my sincerity and my embarrassment, and because she loved me as her own, she bailed me out by taking the gift. She knew I was innocent and sincere, so she said she would make sure that Lena received my present. I could almost feel the pity she had for me as I turned and slowly walked away. If that gift meant nothing to Lena, it meant the world to her mother. She seemed proud to accept my gift for her daughter.

I noticed that Lena's list of victims from Tucson were all there. They were like ants waiting for sugar to fall on a picnic table. I wished everyone a merry Christmas and was on my way. I was glad Lena wasn't available, because for some reason I started trembling, and I couldn't stop. I would have been too nervous to speak.

I had stepped outside to return home when Lena came to the door and shouted, "Wait!"

As I turned she came towards me quickly and slammed the gift into my chest, and without any explanation she shouted, "Give it to Earley. You seem to care more about her."

The tears slowly began to manifest themselves in my eyes as she slammed the door when she re-entered the house. I stood there thinking, *What have I done to this person to deserve this response?* God interpreted my tears, because only God can understand the language of tears. He reached within me and kept my heart from breaking apart. He gathered my tears in a bottle; if only they were as precious to others as they are to God.

I turned and slowly walked away, thinking about the moment and wondering what had I done to perpetrate such rudeness. I think when we are lavished with accolades we often forget where we come from. I knew where I had come from, and I knew who I was, but most important, even then, I knew where I was going. I also knew that she lived in the Toe and chopped cotton just like the rest of us. A year ago she was unnoticed, now she was the center of attention, but she was no different than any of the other girls. Her daddy may have had a better job than our fathers, but that didn't make her any better than the rest of us. It didn't affect Syl, her brother, who was always just one of the Toe Boys, and never thought himself to be any better. It didn't affect the other family members; we all treated each other with love and kindness, so why did it affect her so? Perhaps it was as Solomon said, "*For jealousy is the rage of a man: therefore he will not spare in the day of vengeance*" (Proverb 6:34, KJV). Perhaps I should have said something at that moment, because it is written, "*Open rebuke is better than secret love*" (Proverb 27:5, KJV).

I remembered while picking cotton I had helped Earley, but I had done the same for Lena. Now I understood Solomon when he said, "*Wrath is cruel, and anger is outrageous; but who is able to stand before envy?*" (Proverb 27:4, KJV). Again I can recall the scripture: "*it is better to dwell in the wilderness than with a contentious and angry woman*" (Proverb 21:19, KJV). This guy Solomon had over a thousand wives and concubines, so he must have known what he was talking about.

I decided if that was what she wanted, that was what I was going to do. I took the gift to Earley's house and knocked on the door. When she saw me, she was shocked, but very courteous and pleasant.

I said, "Merry Christmas, I just wanted to give this to you to let you know I care."

It was the wrong thing to do, pretending I had bought it for her, but I did it and was happy about it. Her response told me that was where I should have come in the first place.

She became speechless and just stood there. I gazed into her eyes, and then I walked slowly away. She was so beautiful standing there, and she wore innocence like a tailored garment. I had only taken a couple of steps when I stopped and turned to see if she was still there and she was. She was standing there with the moonlight on her face, and it was at that moment that I realized I had done a good thing. She deserved it, because she appreciated it.

I also realized that at that moment with the moonlight in her face she was extremely beautiful. Her eyes filled with tears that glistened in the light, and her countenance was seared in my mind. I felt bad to have given her a secondhand present, because she was worthy of something better.

The next day the word was out that I was in love with Earley. If giving her a gift causes that sort of rumor, I'm glad I didn't shake her hand, or we would have had to set a wedding date. If I had kissed her that night, then I would have had to start picking a name for the child.

I don't know what Lena was doing to get those kinds of gifts from the guys in town, but the boys in the Toe who were my age were still wondering how to kiss a girl without fainting. The only girl who I ever got close to was Jessie and that was mostly holding her hand and dreaming. I was too young and innocent to even have an illicit dream. Perhaps Lena was innocent as well, and was simply taking advantage of the attention.

I walked Earley home several times from school, but no lights flashed nor did any bells start ringing when I held her hand. I never saw pink clouds overhead, nor did I ever hear violins playing. One night I realized that I was still thinking about Lena, and I didn't know why. She had gone from being my buddy to someone who seemed to despise my presence. I thought the world of her, but again I guess it was a one-sided friendship and only my side was friendly. She had gone from being a little girl to a young lady overnight. She also went from being pleasant to having an attitude. It must have been all the attention she was getting. It was evident that her attitude was taking away from her looks. I was about to learn that inner beauty prevails over outer beauty always.

I had never thought of myself as being a horrible person, so to have someone feel so negatively towards me was difficult to swallow, and it motivated me to try and be a better person.

I walked Earley home one night, and as we approached the door of the house the moon was shining in her face. Her face lit up with the soft glow of the moonlight, and she was so very attractive at that moment. It became a Kodak moment in my mind and will be there forever. I wanted to hold her close and slightly put my lips to hers, but my heart started beating so fast I thought it was going to explode in my chest. I was embarrassed, because my heart beat so loud I thought she heard it, and it beat so hard I thought she could feel it through my shirt.

That night I saw her beauty with my eyes, but I could not see it with my heart. As we came closer I couldn't feel her breath upon my face, because we had both stopped breathing. I thought we had better do something or we would both faint from lack of oxygen. I was about to kiss her, and she was shaking as much as I was, then I heard a voice, "Earley, honey, it's time to come in."

I was so frightened by the unexpectedness of the voice that I pulled away from her embrace and nervously said good night. I left without a kiss and walked through the dark of night slowly to my house, thinking about the opportunity I had missed, and what it would have been like to feel the touch of her lips next to mine. I went to bed that night still feeling her next to me and smelling her fragrance.

When school resumed I went to a dance at the school in the Blue Lizard, which was my car that I had to drive on the back roads because it had no tags. When I got there, of course, Lena was there and that made me happy enough to get set up for another fall. Boys were dancing with her, and she would embrace them on the slow songs, but whenever I asked for a dance she would push me away to arm's length as if I were a leper. Finally it got to a point that she would dance with anyone but me. Earley was there and when we danced she trembled in my arms, but my mind and my heart were on that which I could not have.

I left the dance that night and I went to my car and cried. I tried so very hard to stop the tears from falling, but I could not. It was like God was emptying my soul of all the tears that I had held back from a lifetime of sad moments. I was so dejected and felt so rejected that I thought it would be better to die than to go on living. I thought to myself, *Is there a person out there for me? God, where is she and what will she be like?*

After the tears had fallen and the reservoir was dry, I made a vow to myself and to my God. No more girls, just sports and my education. The only girl I would look at would be the one God personally sent to me. I knew that one day I would rise above the pain, but at that moment it was unbearable. So I destined myself to wait for "the one."

Lena probably never thought twice about the damage she had done to my soul. I knew that one day the very person who Lena loved would put her through the same hell. You can't treat a person the way she did and not reap what you sow.

There is a scripture in the Bible that says, "*...For whatsoever a man soweth, that shall he also reap*" (Galatians 6:7, KJV).

Life is a wheel that keeps turning and what goes around will come around.

CHAPTER ELEVEN

A Prelude to Death

My sister Kitty Mae had been a tomboy all her life. When she got older she would wear boy's clothes and never seemed to care for boys. I remember my sister Mary straightening and curling her hair in a feeble attempt to make her something she wasn't. Kitty Mae would dress like a girl and wear her hair with curls just to entertain us and allow us to fantasize. She never kept it that way for long.

Kitty Mae lived in California and the gay lifestyle there was an open door. We children didn't know what gay meant, and I don't even think the word homosexual was a part of the adult nomenclature. Of course, during that time the word gay simply referred to someone who was happy and full of fun.

Kitty would only visit for a while. She must have known that Mama believed it was morally wrong, and so did the rest of the Toe. She would always bring me toys and gifts, because I was her favorite little brother. The other problem in her life was that she was addicted to heroin. It showed whenever she visited, because things would come up missing. Drugs do have a way of making themselves a priority in the lives of those addicted. The longer she stayed, the more transparent she became. I guess when she had embarrassed herself enough or her conscience started getting the best of her, she would find a way to get back to California. She made her home there, and I supposed she felt more at ease with her peers.

I figured that inevitably she would pay the ultimate price for her addiction.

One day I overheard my parents trying to decide who would go to California and bring back something that belonged to Kitty Mae. I couldn't figure out what they were talking about until my older sister LV took the trip and came back with Kitty's son. His name was Chris. Kitty Mae had sent him home for Mama to raise. I suppose when you run out of money even a gay woman will sleep with a man to get drugs. Chris (Pooh) and Frankie (Tater) grew up in our house and were like younger brothers, except they got plenty of the attention since they were younger. I must admit my mother spoiled those kids to the point that when they grew up they never recovered. They seemed to think that everyone owed them a living and always looked for the easy way out, even if it was illegal. As they would get older they would spend most of their lives behind bars. Both of them were destined to be institutionalized.

One day I got so frustrated that I boldly enlightened my dad of my pitiful situation.

I belted, "How come I go to school and get good grades and no one ever says anything? It's like you expect me to do without things, get good grades, be a good child and there is never any encouragement! I have been on the honor roll and the only person who congratulated me was Mother Hall,"Cleo and Jerry's guardian. "She cooked me a banana pudding, but you and Mom are so busy spoiling Frankie and Chris, you haven't even noticed."

I stood boldly before Dad as I continued, "My bicycle is made from scrap parts and my friends are riding new bikes or riding on motor scooters, but me, I have to make use of used junk!"

My dad never said a word. I never thought that what I had said touched him so deeply. He just looked at me with a countenance that hid his true feelings. I don't think my father even knew what the honor roll was, but he sensed it was something important. He had finished the first grade and my mother had finished the third. They had no knowledge of the grade system, and all they wanted to hear was that we passed from one grade to the next.

I went to school the next day and when I got home my dad called me to come to the back of the house. I knew it was the result of my boldness the day before. I was ready to take my punishment because it was worth it just to let my parents know how I felt. I stepped around the corner and there was my dad with his hands behind his back. I knew he had a belt or something so I prepared myself and approached him like a man. He then took his hands from behind his back and reached out with an open palm. I jumped back but then thought, *How can I be punished with something he can hold in the palm of his hand?*

He took a step towards me and said, "Here, it's yours!"

Again, I took a step back, apprehensive of his intent. In the palm of his hand was a single key. He put it in my hand and closed my fingers around it. He walked around behind me and put both hands on my shoulders and pointed me to an object that was covered with a blanket. He pushed me towards the item and then walked around me.

There was a smile on his face when he said, "Well, what do you think?"

I had no idea what he was talking about until he pointed in the direction of the covered item next to the wall of the house. I looked and I could not believe what I saw. I thought, *Oh my God!* I ran and jumped into his arms and we embraced. Tears were rolling down both our cheeks, and I ran to my gift, yanked the cover off and started yelling, "Yes, yes, yes!" My dad had bought me a Harley-Davidson motorcycle.

I couldn't believe my eyes, and I will never forget that day. It was one of the happiest days of my life. When I showed my motorcycle to the rest of the Toe Boys, I was the proudest son in the world. I knew my father loved me dearly and to buy this gift was not necessary to prove it. I would have loved my dad without the motorcycle. Little did I know that was the last gift I would ever receive from my father. In just a few months he would be gone forever.

I was so happy that I accepted a challenge from Missionary Walker about going to church. She could cook the best apple pie in the world, and she promised me if I came to her church revival, she would give me some apple pie afterwards. Nothing was going to keep me away from Missionary Walker's apple pie.

When I walked through the door of the church, all I could think about was apple pie. I enjoyed the service and the preacher really preached that night. Then came the altar call, so I went up and kneeled down. I really wanted to show how sincere I was, so I could get the apple pie.

My sister Mary had given her life to Christ and was praying over me.

My sister Lou was pretending like always to have something she didn't. If the girl wasn't telling a lie, she was acting a lie. Whenever Mary would tell me to give myself to the Lord and say thank you Jesus, I would cry out in sincerity. When Lou came around, she brought the Devil with her, and all I could think about was apple pie and choking Lou.

Lou would whisper in my ear, "Nigga, I know you're here just for the pie and you're not fooling me. Now, say thank you Jesus, you hypocrite."

When she would walk away from me, I really felt like praising God and the first thing I did was to thank Him for moving her from my presence.

I had been on my knees almost an hour when I decided to really get serious and do as Mary had requested. I asked Christ forgiveness and asked for his mercy and grace.

I prayed, "Lord, forgive me for my sins, and, Lord, if you are really here, show me."

The moment I said that, I had a vision and I found myself kneeling at the foot of a hill. I could still hear my sister praying over me, but I was no longer in the Toe. I didn't know where I was, and I was afraid. I looked up from my kneeling position at the bottom of the hill, and to my disbelief, I saw three crosses, but my attention was on the one in the middle. It was somehow very special. I thought to myself, *What is going on? Where am I?* Something terrible had happened there, and it started getting dark all around me, but the cross in the middle stood out. Oh my God, what was going on? I had seen this place before or I had read about this, but I couldn't figure it out. I wondered, *What happened to the people who were in church, where did they go?* I stared at the cross in the middle and something started to happen. Something moved from the cross. It was a dark cloud of smoke in the shape of a huge ball, and it came rolling towards me. The sound was like the humming of a thousand volts of electricity. I was so afraid. I had to get up and run, or it would hit me as I kneeled. I couldn't get up fast enough, because it was upon me before I could turn to run, and my body became numb. It was the result of all that electricity all over my body. It was on my skin, and I could feel it begin to penetrate into my bones. It was like being shocked with electricity beyond measure. I screamed for help, and I tried to talk, but I could not. It overwhelmed me and as it covered my body it sounded like a million bumblebees. I had to get back to the little church! God, where was it?

Then at the blinking of an eye and as quick as a snap of the finger, I was back at the church.

I was on my feet saying, "Thank you, Jesus. Thank you, Jesus."

I tried to talk but the words wouldn't come out right. The words I tried to speak were not the ones that come from my mouth. I begin to speak in other tongues, and I knew what I was thinking, but it never came out in English, but an unknown tongue. I thought if I could make it to the door and get outside, all this would stop, but the closer I got to the door the more overwhelmed I was. The power that was upon me would not allow me to grab the doorknob. Each time I reached for it, I begin to spend around in a circle, faster and faster.

My sister Mary was still with me saying, "Let go and let God!"

What did she mean? I didn't have God, God had me. I thought to myself if ol' crazy Lou touched me I could come out of this, but I could not feel her presence. I continued fighting in the spirit, but Mary's words finally hit me like a bolt of lightning. Finally I let go and allowed the Spirit to have His way.

I cried out, "Lord, if you need somebody, I'll go."

Suddenly there was joy within me, and I found the greatest inner peace that I had ever felt in my life. It was as refreshing as a summer's rain. It was like the coolness of the rain had fallen upon me, and I was being cleansed. The cleansing pierced my soul and penetrated my spirit. I opened my eyes, which I thought were already open. People around me begin to come into focus, and I thought they were so beautiful. Their smiles shined like the sun, and I could feel the warmth and love that surrounded me. I knew something drastic had happened because even Lou looked good. I took a deep breath and it was pure oxygen. I didn't ever want to sleep because when I woke up, I was afraid this would all be a dream. It was like that old Negro spiritual that said, "I looked at my hand and they looked new, I looked at my feet and they did too."

Missionary Walker offered me some apple pie, but what I had received that night, no pie could match it. I was full, and I hadn't eaten; my thirst had been satisfied, and I had nothing to drink; I had no fear, just a feeling of peace and no need, just Godly contentment.

After church I found that I couldn't even kill a fly. I found myself trying to shoo the fly out of the church house instead of killing it.

I told Mama, as we walked home that night together, "Don't step there." I pointed to the ground in the dark and said, "There's an anthill there."

I could not bear the thought of them being crushed by our footsteps. You may never believe this, but allow me to repeat myself, *even Lou looked beautiful to me that night.*

When I awoke the next morning, I realized it was no dream. I believed I had been in the presence of God, but where was I? I knew that this was the beginning of the rest of my life, and only God knew what was ahead for me.

That Monday I took off from school and went to town to get a haircut and to buy some clothes. My mom had given me some money, and I rode the bus all by myself. I completed what I had gone to do and found that I had lots of time left before the bus to the Toe was scheduled to leave. I decided to go to the movies. The name of the movie was *Ben Hur* and I had never seen it before, so why not?

I was amazed about the special effects and the story. I found tears flowing from my eyes as I watched the scene when Christ was being nailed to the cross. It was then that I remembered I had been there before. That was where I was the other night. I was at the crucifixion of Christ. Oh my Lord, I saw the cross where Christ was nailed. I saw Jesus and He was on the cross in the middle. Tears were flowing now like a flood from the depth of my soul. I could not stop myself, vehemently I wept. Others were staring at me, wondering what was wrong. I saw the waters in the movie that carried the blood of Christ into the creeks and healed the family that had leprosy. I thought about my healing as a child and the many afflictions God had delivered me from. The Holy Spirit was bringing all these things to my remembrance.

Again, my soul cried out, "Thank you, Lord!"

I knew now where God had taken me that night in the church. I knew that he had only confirmed that there was a calling upon my life, but to do what? Why did I see these things? I knew Mama would have the answer, but I couldn't ask, because what if it was the Death Angel talking to me? Mama had always said there was a calling on my life. Was there something I was supposed to do? I thought to myself, *I can never tell anyone about this*. What would the boys in the Toe think, if I told them about these things? God forbid, they would think I had lost it. I thought within myself, *One thing I know, there is a God and anyone who says different is a liar.* I returned home that day with new knowledge and a better understanding. I had stood in the presence of God and had kneeled before the crucifixion of His Son.

I prayed in my room that night, "Now, O God, where will you lead me, where will I go and what do you want me to do?"

The Spirit brought to my remembrance what I had said, "Lord, if you need somebody, I'll go." Suddenly, there was such an inward peace within my soul. I whispered, "Here am I, Lord, send me to the valley, to the mountaintops, over the land and across the sea, send me!"

It was with all sincerity that I lifted my eyes unto heaven and said, "Lord, without You I can do nothing, but with You, I can do all things. My life is in your hands."

CHAPTER TWELVE

Transition

The transition came slow from junior high to high school. My freshman year was a year of grieving, but I made it.

I went out for football and made the varsity team as well as having to play on the freshman team and the junior varsity. I remember the first day of practice I thought I would die. I had never run so much in all my life. All the upperclassmen were calling me rookie and saying the practice was the easiest they ever had.

I thought, *My God, if that was easy, I'm a dead man. I will never be able to make this team.*

While I'm sitting there taking in all their mocking and gesturing, Paul, Cleo's brother, came and sat next to me. Paul looked at me and he saw the doubt that was on my face.

He shouted, "That bal' head White man tried to kill us. I have never had to practice that hard on the first day since I have been playing. If we would have had to run any farther I would have died right there on the field."

So, I asked him if practice was always this hard.

"Are you crazy," he belted, "if it was I wouldn't be here! Coach is just trying to see who's got it and who don't. I guess we've got it, because we made it." He turned and pointed to the guys who were trying to discourage me and said, "Those fools who are talking about how easy it is won't be here tomorrow."

Sure enough, the next day they were turning in their uniforms, but Paul continued to encourage me. I was able to hang in there only because he saw another Toe Boy needed encouragement and he gave it. It was an indication that the spirit of the Toe Boys connected with each other.

Prior to the season, Paul would come by the house and we would jog and run through the desert. We practiced hard on the field and off the field. He would take me down to the river and we would run in the sand to strengthen our legs for endurance. Once we jogged to the bottom of the mountain in the Toe.

When we got there, Paul asked, "Are you ready?"

"Ready for what?" I responded.

"We're gonna climb this mountain!" he shouted.

"Fool," I replied. "You can't climb this mountain, it's too big."

I don't think he heard me, because he had already started climbing. So, the race was on. After about a half hour we reached the top.

Just as I was about to catch my breath, he yelled, "The race isn't finished until we reach the bottom!"

"Reach the bottom!" I exasperated. "I just got to the top!"

I could see that he was oblivious of my statement and was plotting his course down the mountain.

"Let's go! Let's go! Let's go!" he blurted.

When we reached the bottom, we were both exhausted. I caught my breath and found a rock big enough to sit on.

"I'll race you home!" I heard him holler.

I shouted, "You have got to be out of your cotton-picking mind!"

This was not a hundred-yard dash. We were four miles from the house. We ran and we ran and it seemed like an eternity.

When we got to the house, he said, "Don't forget tomorrow."

By the time the first game came around, I was starting on the varsity team with Paul. They called him "Twinkle Toes" because the boy could run like the wind and go through defenders like a gazelle. This was his time; we were in his shadow. I was in the best shape of my life and so was Paul. I called him Harve, because his middle name was Harvey. Man, we worked in the cotton fields all day and ran all night. Our high school had never seen such athletes as the ones who came through the Toe during that time period.

My freshman year in sports was a growing and learning experience. I was the starting defensive back with Paul who played both ways. I had been selected to play on both the varsity and the freshmen team.

My freshman year was Gootee's senior year. Now Gootee was a good football player, but the boy was blind without his glasses. If you gave him the ball and pointed him in the right direction it was hard to stop him before he got to the other goal line. Ol' Cadillac described Gootee as being "damn near smart." It was Gootee who taught me how to do math. He was good at teaching fractions and percentages, and I took advantage of his knowledge.

Our biggest problems came from within the team. The White players were fine, but the Mexican players didn't think we were their equals. They refused to share a room with us when we traveled overnight. They seemed to think more highly of themselves than they should have. Can you believe that? They had the audacity to look down on us. My father had told me, *You never look down on a man unless you're picking him up!*

The Black and White athletes got along well, but the Mexicans were creating a dissonance by being prejudiced and discriminating. That was like a light-skinned Black calling a dark-skinned Black a nigger. I think the Mexican players had a difficult time trying to figure out where they belonged. They wanted the benefits of being a minority, but they wanted to pass for White. They would even list themselves as White on applications. I believe they felt this was the way they were supposed to act towards us to be accepted by White America.

Well, it didn't work. They isolated themselves by their discriminative tactics and their racist attitudes. Neither the Black nor White athletes had much respect for their actions. We loved them as fellow athletes, but we hated the spirit that was in them. It is written: "The White Man's happiness cannot be purchased by the Black Man's misery" (Frederick Douglass in *The North Star*). It was also written, "When people like me, they tell me it is in spite of my color; when they dislike me, they point out that it is not because of my color" (Frantz Fanon, *Black Skin, White Masks*).

Dr. King was fighting for the rights of all the forgotten people, not just Black America. Instead of coming together, so we could have power, the Mexicans were creating schisms. They should have known that "*a house divided against itself can not stand*" (Matthew 12:25, KJV).

Paul was a leader on the team and was a tremendous athlete. Later in life he would prove himself in professional sports. He was always positive and his famous word was "A-l-l-r-i-g-h-t." He would watch other players do things on the field, and he would always say, "That's all right." He was very nice to people and very respectful. He would always make light of a bad situation, and when you were too tired or angry to smile, he always seemed to pull a smile out of you. Sometimes all he did was look at you and smile. That was enough to get a response.

There was a time when I saw him stand his ground for the team. We were in a Mormon town and we were in a restaurant about to eat our pre-game meal. They brought our steaks to us almost raw, and we ordered them well done. We didn't care too much about eating meat that was covered with blood. The restaurant employees did this in an effort to show their contempt for us eating in their restaurant, and it exemplified their racism. This was in the town of Safford, Arizona.

Paul called the waiter to our table and asked him what kind of meat it was. The waiter in his arrogance told Paul, "It's beef," thinking Paul was ignorant of what kind of meat was set before him. Perhaps he may have thought we had never had a steak before.

Paul stood up and yelled, "Watch this!"

He grabbed his steak knife and stabbed the meat with such force that the knife broke through the plate and stuck into the table.

He looked up at the waiter and shouted in the presence of all the customers, "There, I just killed it, now you go cook it!"

They were so embarrassed that they took our steaks back and cooked them the way we desired.

CHAPTER THIRTEEN

Papa's Home Going

My father was a hard-working man and spent most of his time working. My father was about six foot two or three and about a hundred and eighty pounds. He started losing weight and coughing a lot. He got so sick he was admitted to the hospital. Once they let him come home, and he was in a wheelchair and was connected up to all kinds of tubes. It was a frightening sight. I remember his friends would come over, and when my mother wasn't in the room, they would sneak him a drink or offer him a smoke. He would initially refuse, but after consistent badgering he would accept. I thought, *What kind of friends are these?*

I do believe that it was his choice to receive it or refuse it. His condition began to get worse, and he was back in the hospital again. He would ask for me because I was the only one who could make him laugh. The irony of this was, when he laughed, it hurt. When I would visit my father, I could see that he was skin and bones. Papa weighed about ninety-five pounds and you could see his ribs. Even though it hurt him to laugh, he always wanted me to humor him. This mountain of a man had become an anthill and this well of water had become a dried-up brook. It was a heartbreaking sight, seeing him wither before our eyes.

My dad, who said he didn't believe in God, had started asking for prayer. The saints would go visit him and pray for him. I don't know if

Dad accepted Christ, but I was told he did while on his deathbed. One thing I do know is that I wouldn't want to rely on deathbed salvation, and then, just before I die, God said, "NO!"

I was very angry with my father during his illness. I missed him and needed him to be there for me, but he was too sick to go to any games. He had been disabled from his illness for almost a year. He wasn't there when I made the winning basket, or the touchdown that put us ahead, nor was he there for me to ask questions about growing up. I never got the story about the birds and the bees, so I had to lean to my own understanding.

I knew nothing about his side of the family and I never met any of his sisters or brothers. He told me about his involvement in World War I, and how he had fought overseas. He told me once that he was in an Army jeep that was blown up by a grenade, and it resulted in a broken collarbone. He showed me how the bone stood out, because it was never set correctly. He said his father Scott Colter and his mother, Emma Porter, were either his real parents or adopted parents. He said he was born in Virginia and raised up in Crockett, Texas.

My sister said Dad's family once owned a funeral home that was burnt down when he was a child. To this very day, my father's life and relatives remain a mystery to me. My hair was reddish, and I was told that my father's hair was red, before it turned gray, and then he became bald. He had come from a family of people with red hair.

I had just gotten my license and Mom wanted me to take her to visit Dad. I was so proud, and I wanted to show him. He had allowed me to drive to the garbage dump on the back roads, and to hunt as long as I stayed in the desert area. I had driven the Blue Lizard, my brother's junk vehicle, which I had brought back to life, but I only drove on the back roads. Now I could drive on a real road, and I wanted to thank him for letting me drive places while he was sick.

Mom and I dropped the others off at my sister LV's house and we went to the hospital to see Dad. We got to the hospital and entered his room, but he wasn't there. They were always moving him to different rooms.

We met his nurse in the hallway and she said, "Oh good, you're here."

She gave us his clothes and told us as soon as they gathered up his other belongings they would give it to us.

We had no idea where they had taken him, so Mom asked, "Where is he?"

The lady responded, "Don't you know, he is dead? Your husband died early this morning. Didn't the sheriff tell you?"

I was standing behind my mother when she said, "No, no, no!"

She exhaled and collapsed. She fell backward and I grabbed her as we both melted to the floor of the hospital. I never thought my father would ever not be with us. The nurses and doctors started apologizing to us and said the sheriff was told early that morning to give us the death notification. Apparently he decided to do it later that day after we had left home. The sheriff being White and we being Black, well, that could have had some bearing on why it wasn't urgent information to him. I took Mama back to LV's and I don't know how I was able to see through all the tears. The thing that bothered me the most was, I never got the chance to tell my daddy goodbye.

We told the rest of the family and they cried, but they seemed to have expected Dad to die. No one would tell me anything when I would ask about his illness.

When I found out that he had died from cancer and it was a result of smoking cigarettes, I became very angry with him. He couldn't have stop smoking just for me? My dad chose a cigarette over me? My own family wouldn't tell me the truth about Dad's condition. Was it because I was the youngest or was it Dad's secret? If only I would have known that he had but a short time I would have done everything differently. I don't think I would have left his side, if only I knew.

The Toe Boys were there for me, and their compassion reached way down at times to pick me up. Their love brought me from the valley of despair to ground level. We vowed to always be there for each other. We cut our wrists and shared blood, like the Indians did in the movies. We would make a small cut on our arm, and we would grab each other's arm and match each cut to the other and hold that position until we felt the blood had mixed. We became blood brothers, and nothing and no one could separate us. I remember Frank being the first to cut his arm and then I cut mine. We wrapped our arms together for a brief time, thinking that our blood had mixed. It was from that point on that we considered ourselves more than friends, but blood brothers. It was a bond that would last a lifetime.

There were times, soon after my father's death, I would get Dad's shotgun and go hunting just to get away. One day I found myself alone in the desert with Dad's old shotgun, just sitting on the riverbank. I had no desire to shoot anything, I just wanted to be there with something that belonged to him and hold it close to me. I took out a pencil and a small notebook and I wrote a poem entitled "Tell me why, a father must die?"

I have searched throughout this life of mine
Just to find out why
Someone so Divine as Almighty God
Could let my father die
I've often wondered when my time has come
Would I leave behind a weeping child?
Just as he had done
Would I be loved while dead for years?
I wonder how many would actually shed tears
It's not of me that my heart now cry
It's about a loving father
And why he had to die
I remember the wonderful times
That he and I once had
He made me so very happy
There were never times to be sad
He would take me on a trip
Whenever my day was a bore
He would tell me all about God
And that I should love him more
Someday son he would quietly say
My time will soon come
And I'll pass away
You shall live on and on
To take our family through
All the hard times and unhappy days
Just as I would do
I can still hear his voice
Yes, it was a lovely sound

Of a father that meant the world to me
Even after being placed beneath the ground
God I love you both so much
But I just don't understand why
Someone so Divine as You
Could let my father die
I would give anything to have my father here
I could tell him how much I miss him
Whenever he's not near
I could show him how much I love him
In each and every way
Just as he would show his love
Before that awful day
People would often see me cry
And talked to me as a friend
There's no need for you to stop living
Because his life has end
In a quiet way, I would sadly say
I just want to be with my father
Now tell me, is that a sin?
Whenever I ask questions about the death of my father
Some said it was bad luck
Others walked away, with nothing to say
Others said wait and grow up
Well, now I'm a man and I still don't understand
So will someone please tell me why
Someone so Divine as Almighty God
Would let my father die
When my time comes
Maybe I will have a son
Who will someday become a man
And when he asks why a father must die
Please try to explain
Tell him how God created the heaven and earth
In only six short days
And how he loved this world he built

In so many different ways
Tell him God created Adam and Eve
And how life begin
Tell him we could have had everlasting life
But Satan tempted man to sin
Tell him about God's only son
Who was nailed to a cross to die
So that every child who is born
Could breathe the breath of life
So when my son asks why, a father must die
This is all you have to say
The God that giveth thee love and life
Can surely taketh away

My brother Butch (Junior) was in the military and we had sent him the news of Dad's passing. He missed the funeral and came in later that day. We figured it was the Army's red tape that caused him to be late. (Later in life this become somewhat of a trend, because he would miss a lot of funerals.) He later got out of the military and came home just to steal the family's car and leave us without transportation.

I am reminded of what Mom would always say, "If it ain't one thing, it's another." It seems that the people you think are coming to help you are the ones who come to hurt you or bring you down. I loved my brother, but he was niggardly and would sell you into slavery to make a dollar. He was indeed the epitome of selfishness and egotism.

With my father gone and my mother struggling to make ends meet, it created in me a desire to succeed. Though I was the youngest son, I became the man in the house. I found myself getting involved in all sports. Anything that could take up time was good enough for me. I played football, basketball, baseball and ran track. I also trained to box, and I would finish one practice and go to the gym in town until eleven o'clock at night.

One day my brother came home in another car. Apparently he had sold ours and bought himself one. He said our car was haunted. He said he would be driving down the road and the car would just stop for no reason.

If he let someone else get in to drive, the car would start, but not with him. He would turn the key off and the car would keep running. He sometimes took the key out of the ignition and as he walked away the car would stop running.

Mama said that Daddy might have had something to do with it. She said she had a dream about Dad and he had the car keys in his hand. She was telling him to give them to my brother Butch (Junior), but Dad said no, and in the dream he said, "Give them to Lace."

Mom said she didn't understand why Dad would want me to have the keys instead of Junior, because he was the oldest. After he stole the car and left us stranded, she realized what the dream was all about. She said it was God, not my father, warning her not to give him the keys. I believe my brother's perception of the car being haunted was only a reflection of his guilt, and a well-needed tune-up. But God does work in mysterious ways.

CHAPTER FOURTEEN

The Legacy Begins

My father had passed, it was during track season, and my first year in high school was coming to a close. I was done with girls but I would talk to Earley once in a while. Lena, well, that was another story. Once she came over to the house and I was asleep. Lou woke me up and said they needed some change because they were going to the store to buy something. I was half asleep so I told Lou to get the money from my pants near the bed. The next thing I remember was Lou coming into my room being boisterous and throwing the money back at me while I lay in the bed.

She then told me, in her normal nasty and obnoxious manner, "Lena said she didn't want your money. Why don't you give it to Earley like you do everything else."

I could never understand that if she had all these boyfriends and all this attention, why would she be concerned about me talking to Earley? Nevertheless, I loved her as a friend in spite of her attitude towards me. She was like a sister, and it seemed that when those feelings crossed over the line was when things changed in our relationship. My advice is never fall in love with your friend. Of course, I never dismissed the thought that Lou could have been lying, and Lena had said no such thing.

Lena was so capricious that I never knew which Lena would show up when I saw her. One night she came over and spent the night with my sister Lou. I went into my sister's room, and Lena and I got in a conversation about Earley. She was combing her hair and seemed frustrated with the results, so I took the comb and started combing. I talked to Lena and combed her hair almost all night long. This was the Lena who had stolen my heart, and as we talked about Earley, I thought about Lena. My mind and my heart reunited with the Lena who had been my childhood friend. I thank God for that warm moment, and the compassion she showed by listening and being concerned. We talked about personal relationships, and I recorded that night in my diary. I asked her about her two boyfriends from town.

"Lena, I know those boys are probably in love with you, or they wouldn't travel such a distance to see you. I also know that you must like them to go out with them so regularly, but are you in love with either of them?"

Her instant reply was, "No, I'm not!"

I knew that one of them was a muscle builder and perhaps it was his physical appearance that attracted her. It is written, "*Man looketh on the outward appearance, but the Lord looketh on the heart*" (1 Samuel 16:7).

Later that morning I retired to my room and thought about our conversation. My mama summarized Lena in one statement: "It's hard to be humble when you're pretty!" But there were lots of pretty girls in the Toe, and they were humble.

I know that we boys all accepted each other as friends and the only thing that got in the way were girls. They never came between us boys, but the girls in the Toe were always feuding over something. I think the girls were jealous of how the boys felt about each other. We had an intimacy that went beyond friendship to brotherly love. We would have died for one another if necessary. The love we had for each other allowed us to overlook each other's faults. The girls could not bring themselves to care enough about each other to see beyond their hang-ups. It is written, "*…above all things have fervent charity among yourselves: for charity shall cover the multitude of sins*" (1 Peter 4:8, KJV).

My sister Mary, Cleo's sister Irene, Frank's sister Ester, and James's sister Georgia seemed to have the same bond as we did, but the rest showed no real commitment of friendship. The girls competed against each other over boys and were always in each other's business. The older girls switched boyfriends back and forth like we traded marbles. It seemed that they were always fighting and were always in cliques. You never knew who was going with whom that week, and if you really needed to know you just asked Lou.

Football season had approached and we played a game in Wilcox, and Black and White athletes shared rooms, but the Mexicans all slept together. I guess they thought if they roomed with us overnight, they would wake up the next day with dark skin, an overwhelming craving for chicken and watermelon, and a strong craving for chitterlings, instead of menudo.

Frank said, "A Mexican is nothing more than a light-skinned Black man with straight hair, and he speaks another language."

Whatever their perceptions of us and ours of them, racism and bigotry is wrong. I was taught that prejudice is an attitude, but discrimination is an action. It was bad enough dealing with the opposition in each little town, but we had to contend with our own players (Mexican) who were prejudiced and discriminated against us.

Poor Cleo had to bunk with Floyd, and during the night Floyd peed in the bed. Cleo tried to sneak in the bed with Carl, who must have woke up from a nightmare, because he was about to punch him out when Cleo yelled, "Carl, it's me, please don't hit me!"

He explained to Carl that Floyd had wet the bed, and he didn't want to lie down in Floyd's urine. Carl let him in the bed, and from that night on, we knew a secret about Floyd. Hopefully he corrected that problem before he got married later in life. Floyd was also a pathological liar, and I hoped he was delivered from that affliction as well. His twin brother Lloyd gave me that bit of information, and he was a bit more truthful.

Most of the teams we played against were composed of White and Mexican players. I don't remember playing football or basketball against a team in our conference with one Black player on it, except Wilcox, who had one Black player.

We played them in a football game and an opposing player caught a pass and was running down the sidelines with burning speed. The only person in the position to stop him was Cleo. We didn't worry because Cleo was one of the surest tacklers on the team. When Cleo would tackle you, he was like white on rice or stink on do-do. Cleo was defending someone else, but he looked up and saw the boy coming and went after him like a cannonball shot from a cannon. We saw the collision coming, so everybody on the team, even the people in the stands, put their hands over their ears. Folk were holding on to each other, reaching out, grabbing hold to bleachers and tree branches, so they could be anchored down when Cleo hit the boy.

Then something amazing happened, Cleo ran up to the player and just brushed him. Cleo was going in the opposite direction, and the boy on the other team kept right on running toward the goal line. We figured this boy done went over the insanity line. So Frank and I went after the White boy, because we just couldn't let him score and make Cleo look that bad. Man, Frank and I hit him and brought him down on the one-yard line. We jumped up and high-fived each other.

Frank told the boy, "Not here, punk!"

You see, sports were the only place you could talk to White people like that or beat up on them and nobody tried to hang you. I guess that's why we enjoyed it so. It was like society had given us a legal means of whooping White folk for a change. Now this boy was calling us all kind of niggers.

We told him, "Yeah, but you didn't make it, did ya?"

Then Frank made a discovery. "Hey, Codas," he said with a look of astonishment, "he don't got the ball!"

I'm thinking, *Why did we hit this poor boy if he doesn't have the ball?*

Then from the stands came screaming and hollering. Everyone had stood to their feet and was looking at Cleo and cheering. There he was at the other end holding up the football. Cleo had stolen the ball in his brief encounter with the other player, and the player haven't known it. Cleo had scored a touchdown.

This was the second time that Frank had given a diagnosis for Cleo. Frank said that there was a name for Cleo's condition. He said Cleo was a "calypso maniac" but he was a good calypso maniac, whatever that meant. Frank said it was a person who stole stuff and didn't know it. I believe that Cleo was so good he could steal the paint off a wall. By now, we all knew that Frank meant kleptomaniac.

We played a game later that year in Superior, Arizona. We were winning the game and there was no need for us to physically hurt those boys, but Frank was violence personified and was determined to hurt somebody. I think Frank had a little man's complex and that's why he seemed to have a chip on his shoulder.

I went down field to block for Frank, and I hit this poor White boy and put him in a paralytic state. I had stuck him so hard the numbers on his jersey was tattooed on my helmet. He was lying on the ground quivering like he was having an epileptic seizure. I looked up and here comes Frank. There is no one in front of him, but me and the poor boy who I done already paralyzed. Frank ran over to where we were and started at the boy's ankle and ran the length of his body, on his body.

I had to stop Frank and tell him, "Fool, go score the touchdown."

Afterwards I asked, "Why do you do stuff like that?"

"I don't know. Sometimes violence just comes all over me when I think about what they did to us when we were slaves," he belted.

"Fool, you ain't never been no slave, have you lost your mind? Boy, your daddy ain't even old enough to have been a slave," I retorted.

This was not the place for Frank to go off, certainly not in a town that was anti-Black. When the game ended they wouldn't let us use their gym to get dressed. We had to keep on our football clothes and leave the town smelling like a pair of DJ's socks. We kept on our helmets and shoulder pads, because the fans threw rocks and broke out the windows of our bus. Their police department had to escort us out of town with our uniforms on.

On our way home we went through this little town named Coolidge and they truly hated Black people. It was so bad in Coolidge that the Blacks didn't even like each other. We stopped at one of the little hamburger stands and got our dollar-fifty from the coach and went inside. We looked up and here comes all these White boys who we had never seen. They brought with them machetes, baseball bats and some even had guns. They came into the restaurant calling us niggers. Now, we ain't stupid, can't no White person with a gun and big knife incite me by calling me a nigger, and he sure isn't going to provoke me into getting shot.

Ol' crazy Frank called them a nigger right back, then told them that they could have passed for brothers because one of them White boys resembled his daddy. Then they said something they thought was profound. They said our mamas were Negroes and our daddies were lowlifes. Now I have been telling them boys that for years, so they weren't surprised to hear this.

The White boys got angrier because they found it difficult to provoke us, especially when we knew they had guns and knives. This entire incident didn't faze Paul and he was asking everyone who had lost their appetite for their hamburgers.

One of the boys approached Paul and commented, "Hey, boy, didn't you hear me call your mama and daddy niggers?"

Paul walked right up to his face and told him, "Man, as long as you got that gun and that knife, you can call my mama and daddy whatever you want."

We all looked at each other and said, "Dammnn!"

Those boys then got more violent and threatened to shoot us.

Leroy started whispering, "Let's run for it."

I whispered, "Are you crazy?"

I knew he could outrun all of us, and we would be cover for his backside while he was running, so we took all they had to say. When we got back to the bus, Leroy was going around asking who told them all that stuff about our parents.

Everybody at the same time stood up and said, "Shut up, Leroy!"

I tell you, that boy was intelligence challenged. We loved that boy, but it was hard.

Paul's senior year was a tragedy for him, but it was still a great season for us. Paul had broken his leg in practice and couldn't play that year. We carried on and continued winning like never before. Paul handed down to us the will to win and the pride of being who we were. We were not football players or basketball players, nor were we track stars or baseball players. That was what we did, but that was not who we were. We were individuals who loved and respected each other and our parents. We were the Toe Boys growing up.

Paul showed me that the only limitations were the ones we put on ourselves. When Paul left, that's when the dynasty began. Marana High School began its move to become a powerhouse in athletics. Our coaches, who were White, loved us as if we were their own children. Some of them were not old enough to be our fathers, but older brothers. They instilled in us a winning attitude and the will to never give up or give in.

Coach Hawkins said before each game, "You can't win them all if you don't win this one."

The coaches had vowed to help all of us to get into college if we so desired. We were told that we could not make it into college just being good; we had to be the best. If colleges had to choose between Black and White athletes, we couldn't just be better, we had to be the best.

The coaches got us into the best shape of our lives. When other teams were running out of gas in the fourth quarter, we were just getting started. We had not lost a game, and we were on the road to fame.

Our quarterback was a White kid name Richard. Richard was like a brother to us, and his whole family was racially color-blind. We spent the night at his house and would visit from time to time. The thing I liked about Richard was he was always himself. He never tried to be Black, and he never put any emphasis on the fact that he was White. Richard was a person of a different color, but I know that his compassion leaned in our direction. I remember when the Mexican players didn't want to share the same room with the Blacks.

Richard stood up and said, "I'll share a room, what's the big deal?"

Richard's parents didn't teach him prejudice or racism, but there were times when I would hear his father yell to the coaches, "Take them peckerwoods out of there and put in the kids who really want to play," referring to the Black athletes as the ones who really wanted to play.

We went to Benson to play a football game and we knew we were in for a fight. I don't mean the football team, but the fans as well. Whenever we were tackled on the sidelines, they would pour beer in our faces. As we lay on the ground they would bombard you with popcorn and other debris.

They allowed their fans to line up near the sidelines and they would have bicycle chains, brass knuckles and would brandish guns and knives. They would make sure we saw these items whenever we came to their side of the field, and they would threaten to kill us if we scored.

You could hear them yelling, "You niggers better not win this game or it'll be your last!"

We never told the coaches about any of this, and it only motivated us the more. Carl and Frank made tackles on the other team's sideline, and beer and popcorn was thrown in their faces. That was the wrong thing to do because Carl kept going back for more; he had acquired a taste for beer. And Frank was actually picking the popcorn off the grass and eating it in the huddle.

He kept doing it until I told him, “Frank, it’s probably laced with poison.”

Frank started spitting popcorn everywhere. He got scared and started praying aloud, “Lord, don’t let me die!”

I explained to him that I didn’t think he would die and that he needed to get off his knees and get back into the huddle.

Carl, on the other hand, had so much beer thrown in his face that he looked as if he was getting high. Richard was upset with Leroy because he didn’t grease his legs, and his ankle socks kept slipping down, showing how ashy they were. He was always on Leroy and Frank before the games trying to get them to lotion their legs and comb their hair. It must be bad when your White friend got to tell you this. What Richard didn’t know was that those boys had some nappy hair. There wasn’t any grease or lotion powerful enough to keep ash from showing through.

The score was tied and we were running out of time. Richard was a southpaw and could thread a needle with a football at forty yards. He called a play and added to it right there in the huddle. The coach had sent in a pass, but Richard changed it to a draw play. He wanted me to flank out and go down on a pass pattern, but he was going to fake the pass and give it to Leroy on a draw play. I went down and blocked this player and rolled over on him to pin him to the ground. I was lying on my back looking up when I saw Leroy break through the line. Immediately three players from the other team zeroed in on poor Leroy, and I knew it was over for him. They prepared to spear him with their helmets, and I could see this disaster about to unfold before my eyes. I wasn’t in a position to help because he was too far away. They all hit him at the same time, and his helmet flew off his head and went straight up about ten feet in the air. One of his shoes came off and landed on the sideline. All of this was in slow motion, even though it only lasted a couple of seconds. Leroy disappeared, covered by the jerseys of the other team. I knew Leroy was a dead man, but to my surprise the guys that had wrapped him up like a sandwich started peeling off like you would peel a banana. Leroy came out of the crowd running on all threes, without a helmet and with one shoe. He ran seventy yards and scored the winning touchdown.

There was a big fight after the game between the fans. Thank God, no one died. Leroy was our hero and that night belonged to him. Each of us would have our moments in the sunshine from time to time, but that night Leroy took it to another level. His gift of athleticism was manifested in his efforts, and that night, I believe, he was set apart from the rest of us. God had given us grace and mercy, and it was personified in a Toe Boy called Leroy.

The next big game we had was with a team called Ray. We saw the brass knuckles and knives, the chains and the brandishing of weapons like usual. They threw popcorn and beer in our faces and threatened to kill us all, like all the other schools we played. We were having a difficult time with them because they seemed to know where the play was going before we ran it.

We couldn't figure it out until halftime, when Richard's father told the coaches that he overheard them saying that the running backs were telegraphing where they were going before the ball was snapped. They were watching our eyes, and we seemed to look in the direction we were going. When we returned for the second half, Richard would call a play and tell us to look in the direction we were going to go. We did so and sure enough he could tell they were keying on our eyes.

Richard then called a play and told us to look in the opposite direction when we came out of the huddle. I looked to the outside and Richard called a play up the middle. Sure enough, their entire team shifted to one side and was totally out of position. I received the ball and went through a hole that you could have driven a truck through.

Again, Richard told us to look deliberately in the wrong direction. We did and this time Leroy took the ball down field for about twenty yards. The next time it was Cleo's turn, and he took the ball to midfield for another ten. Now, it was my turn again, and after following instructions I took the ball on a handoff up the middle. A player that was about six feet seven inches tall was chasing me, and he was bearing down on me. That is until I shifted gears and left him standing there spitting out grass that my shoes had thrown up. I went fifty yards for the touchdown. This was now my time and all the other players rejoiced with me. The victory was ours, and this was my time for heroics. After crossing the goal line, the entire team was there piling on and celebrating. We now knew the secret and we proceeded on to win the game. The victory was ours and the season ended with us being champions.

Basketball season was rolling around again, and I thought I would ask Earley to a basketball game. I went over to her house and she seemed to have anticipated my arrival. Her mom came to the door and I asked if I could take Earley to the game. Her mom's face lit up and she was beaming with joy for the both of us. Her countenance changed, though, when she directed me to Earley's father to see if it was okay. I could hear his firm resentment from the doorstep.

He said, "Absolutely not! He ain't no good. He'll drop out just like the rest." Of course, it was his son who dropped out to work, not any of us.

He said that I would never amount to anything. I would probably drop out of school any day now, and I was not the type he would let his daughter go out with.

Apparently his neighbor had told him that none of the Toe Boys were any good, and I would probably end up a criminal since my father was dead. I could hear Earley's mother and older sister V arguing my case, but to no avail.

Their next-door neighbor had made it seem that his kids were the only decent children in the Toe. That family had just moved there and knew nothing of the families there, but yet they judged us. The scripture tells us, "*Judge not, that ye be not judged. For with what judgment ye judge, ye shall be judged: and with what measure ye mete, it shall be measured to you again*" (KJV, Matthew 7: 1-2).

He told me to leave and that is what I did. I thought maybe he was right. It seemed that wherever I went doors were closing in my face. I thought to myself, *If there is a God, where is He?*

I went over to Syl's house and Lena wasn't there and that was a relief. Between the two of them, these girls were driving me crazy. They would later prove to be the only negative part of my childhood.

Football had ended and we had a big basketball game coming up that night, and I'd had enough rejection for one day. The Toe Boys were there, and we were talking about the game and trying to get psyched up. I told them about Earley, and they were trying to console me and tell me not to worry. They reminded me of the vow I had made: no more girls.

While we were talking, Syl had this metal clothes hanger and he was doing something with it, but I was not really paying any attention. He then handed this metal hanger to me, and I grabbed it not really thinking. Then it dawned on me that it was red hot. The fool had put it in the fire and handed it to me as a joke. It burned a line across my hand, and I was jumping up and down hollering. I searched until I found a bucket of water and plunged my hand into the water to relieve the pain.

He thought it was very funny until I told him it was my shooting hand, and we had a game in about four hours. Again, my affection for Lena saved his life. I have said this often and I will say it again, if it weren't for Lena, several of us would have killed Syl years ago. I knew that I would probably have to wait in a long line until my turn came, but it would have been worth the wait.

Well, I did what I could to help my hand heal for the game and showed up ready to play.

During the warm-ups, the guys said, "Lace, don't lose it…but look at the entrance."

I was doing layups and as I turned I saw Earley. She was with a boy named Ed. His father had cut me down like a lawn mower so his son could take out my date? The guys were trying all they could to keep me from going over and punching out Ed. He then had the audacity to come to me while I was on the court and tell me she was with him, and though I may have thought she was my date, she was his date tonight. Again I went for him with the intent to take his head off of his shoulders, but Frank grabbed me.

Earley said she came to the game to see me, but I often wondered why she would come with another guy. If she cared about me then why would she come to the game with him? This was starting to get complicated, but I remembered my vow: no more girls, never again.

The game went as planned and we won. Leroy was putting the ball through the hoop like a pro, and Richard was playing like he was Black. The rest of us did our part and later rejoiced in the victory.

Richard came by Cleo's house the next day and we went to a basketball game at the University of Arizona. The U of A won fifty-nine to fifty-one. We had a good time, and it was one of a very few times that I had ever seen a college team play. I kept thinking to myself, *I want to go to college and play sports*. I knew the only way this was possible was by putting first things first. No more girls!

Oh, how soon we forget. The next day Earley gave me a ring and I wore it around my neck on a chain. We made up, and I knew that I cared about her, but I could never tell her to her face. I could write it on paper or even tell others, but I was so bashful I could never tell her. It took me about two months before I was able to give her a petty kiss. I guess I had Lena to thank for going with Earley, because if it weren't for her I would have never made the move.

One day I lost the setting in her ring, and I was so embarrassed, I avoided her as much as possible. Then things got worse: I lost the ring. I would go to the church, and she was there. It seemed that no matter where I went I would see Earley. I finally told her about the ring, and she got angry and wouldn't talk to me. I would see her at different places, and she would walk by me without saying anything. I would go places, because I was told that she wanted to talk to me, but when I got there she ignored me. I think the messengers just wanted a laugh. The entire ordeal was getting out of hand, and my nerves were on edge. The love I once had was starting to turn to disgust and regret.

One day I went to the church where the choir was practicing, and she was there. I saw her walking up to me, and I didn't know what to do, so I froze. She approached me and handed me something and folded my fingers over it and walked away. I figured it was a note telling me to drop dead, or a biological weapon that would kill me within minutes, but instead it was a picture of her. I thought it was very beautiful, but what was written on the other side was even better. She wrote in big letters, "I love you."

It seemed that there wasn't a day that went by that I didn't think of her. She was a very beautiful girl with big dark brown eyes and Black hair that covered a caramel face. She was quiet and very pleasant.

I would go over to Lena's, and we would get in a conversation about Earley. Once she even helped me write a letter to Earley, but what she didn't realize was the words we put on that paper were intended for her.

No matter how much I would convince myself that I was in love with Earley, I could never stop thinking about Lena. It was our friendship that had turned my heart inside out. Lena could be the sweetest person in the morning and by evening she was like sour grapes. I don't know if Lena ever liked me more than for a friend, but I had my suspicions that some of her capriciousness came from being jealous and not because she cared. I do know that of all the years I knew her, and the love that I had for her, never even resulted in a single kiss. The only time I ever embraced her was when we danced and from arm's length.

Lena was a friend, but her friendship was much different than that of the boys. The Toe Boys were not only committed to friendship, but they had integrity. Integrity is the ability to stay committed. Neither Lena nor any of the girls in the Toe had integrity. Their loyalty changed on a daily basis. It was like someone was pulling a light switch on and off.

One day I went to town to visit my sister LV and her son Billy (this was the same Billy who almost died with me in the storm). He introduced me to several girls. One girl named Sandra became a friend. Later we started writing letters to each other, and before you knew it, we were involved in a long-distance relationship. Sandra and I never went any further than writing letters, because we lived too far apart. The letters that she wrote were indeed a great consolation when the girls in the Toe were acting ugly. She actually came to my house once with Lou and we talked. Our relationship was totally friendship, but filled with anticipation of something that would be.

I knew it was Lou's way of perpetrating defecation. She wanted to create a dissonance between Earley and me.

She, of course, told Earley the next day, "Girl, my brother, your so-called boyfriend, had this girl from town in our house and he kissed her and I have no idea what other things they may have done."

That was ol' Lou, in everybody's business. I was able to get beyond Lou's gossip and her accusations of me dating half of the girls in the city of Tucson, Arizona. The problem with Lou was that she was like Floyd: she lied so much she started believing herself.

Basketball ended with us on top and we were ready for track. We went from one sport to another. It was now track season, and we had the fastest guys in the state. The quarter mile relay team and the mile relay team never lost. Leroy was the fastest thing on two feet, and I was second. Cleo and Frank ran the hurdles, sprints and were on the relay teams with Leroy and myself. Leroy would only run fast enough to win, so no one ever knew just how fast he was. All the Toe Boys had their individual events and excelled in them.

One time, we were running the mile relay. When the runner came around to hand off the baton to Carl, he had disappeared. We all started yelling, "Carl, Carl," and he must have heard us because he ran to the track from the desert into his lane and kept running until the baton was handed to him. If you would have looked carefully, you may have seen a bit of toilet paper protruding from his shorts.

We were behind until Leroy, who was filling in for Floyd (thank God), got the baton and almost caught up by passing several runners. He then handed it to me, and the race was on for the finish line. I had a hard time running curves, and I had to turn sideways just to stay in the lane. My heart was beating in overtime mode, and I could see myself passing the guys ahead of me, one at a time. I got to the front of the pack and there was one runner left to catch, but I was running out of time and track. We came around the 330-yard mark of the final lap and hit the straightaway. I saw people jumping up and cheering, but I couldn't hear them. It seemed that I was in another dimension, and all the air in the world was sucked out. I floated beside the runner, and I could see that he too was in another world. I thought to myself, *Please, Lord, just give me the strength to finish.* I saw the finish line, and I willed my body to pass the runner. I crossed the finish line first and immediately I could feel myself returning to this physical world. All the pain and agony of being totally exhausted hit me all at once, and I saw total darkness. The adrenaline rush was fading and I was returning to the state of reality, and I began to feel the ultimate exhaustion and the pain of the race.

For a moment all my strength left me, but before I collapsed, I could feel the support of my teammates holding me up and helping me to stand.

"You did it, you did it! We won!" they shouted.

Lee was the first to come into focus and he yelled, "Codas, you did it, and it was beautiful. Man, you and Leroy ran a perfect race."

I was told that Leroy and I both had run record times in the quarter mile to win that race. All the Toe Boys got in a circle and embraced one another in victory. God had heard my prayer and given me the strength. The heart that the doctors said should have stopped long time ago never gave up, and the feet that were to never walk again had carried us to a victory. The will to win always overcomes the desire to give up.

We became the team to beat in all sports. We continued in victory, meet after meet, and race after race. We had yet to reach our peak, but we were just enjoying the times because we were Toe Boys growing up.

CHAPTER FIFTEEN

Relationships

It was the end of our sophomore year, and the summer was upon us. Swank (Sonny) and Frank had found two girls who were cousins, and they both claimed they were in love. They had one problem: those girls were not allowed to go out unless a sister who was a year older would go and chaperone them. Their answer to this was me. They wanted me to go out with them and be the date for the sister. My immediate answer to this was absolutely not! I didn't want to get stuck with the ugly duckling that always had a good personality, was fun to be with but looked like the Wicked Witch in *The Wizard of Oz*.

They knew the only way to get us together was to trick me. We had a game at the YMCA playing in the summer basketball league. We went to play a game one night, and Sonny brought his girlfriend's sister. Apparently it was the only way her mother would allow her to go out. Now, I'm thinking, I have to put up with a blind date at a time when I had had it with women.

Her name was Shirley, but her family called her Regina, which was her middle name. I was shocked that she wasn't ugly; in fact, she was a very nice-looking girl with a very pleasant and quiet disposition. I thought she had on too much make-up, but I could see that under the unnecessary cosmetics was a beautiful girl. The first opportunity I had I told her I wasn't looking for a girlfriend. I didn't want a girlfriend, and all I wanted to do was play sports and go to college.

It was then that I noticed she had brown eyes and a nice smile. She looked downward, careful not to look me in the eyes, and said softly and in a low voice, "Okay."

When we took them home, I realized they were very poor. I thought country was poor until I met Regina and Debbie (Sonny's girl). We may not have had the best house or the best car, but what we had belonged to us. Those girls were living in a rented house with two small bedrooms and ten people. Their mom was a single parent and struggled to make ends meet. Regina and Debbie would work part time with a plumber name Dudley. The other kids were too young to do anything, other than sleep, eat, use the bathroom and complain.

The older girls were always helping their little brothers and sisters, who never really seemed to care, and thought their compassion should have been automatic. They took love for granted and seemed to forget that we lived in a world where family members were killing each other.

Sonny would make sure I was there whenever the girl's mom demanded they had an escort. We took them out to eat, and it appeared that Regina hadn't eaten all day, judging by the way she was eating. Later that night I asked her why she was so hungry. She said she hadn't eaten in two days, because she wanted to make sure her sisters and brothers had something to eat. She was about five feet two inches tall and weighed ninety-eight pounds. She would go without so they could have something. Again, I reminded her that I wasn't available, because sports were all I needed.

Again she said, "Sure, I know and I understand."

Our night came to an end with her in my arms and a goodnight kiss. On the way home I kept thinking, *That's the first time I have ever felt comfortable with a girl.* When I was around Lena I was a wreck, because you never knew what to expect. With Earley I was always nervous. I guess when you grow up with girls and start liking the one you grew up with, your life is like an open book. With Regina, I could keep secrets, and I would only tell her what I wanted her to know. She wasn't like the Toe Girls, always expecting something from you. They were as capricious as a bad lightbulb. You never knew when they would be on or off or about to blow.

We continued to see each other, but seldom, and only when Sonny and Debbie needed someone to watch over them. After a while we started getting more intimate, and I decided that Regina and I were the ones who really needed the chaperone.

I decided it was getting way out of hand, so I stopped going to town. I then started getting letters telling me how wonderful I was. She wanted me to find my dream and pleaded for me to think about her as I endeavored to reach the mountaintop. I wrote in return, and my letters got a lot mushier than I anticipated. I even told her that I liked her. I asked myself, *What is it about this girl that continues to let me know something eternal is building up inside us?* I always felt she wanted what was best for me even if it meant being without her.

This was starting to get confusing. A girl who put me first, now that was hard to believe. I didn't want any longer to be with Earley, whom I thought was naïve, or Lena who was blowing fuses every other day. I had never been with any girl who didn't have strings attached. Even Jessie came with strings attached, because she was my cousin. I guess you can say that Shirl's package included her family, and many of them needed a reality check.

I had lost my father and Regina (Shirl) had lost her grandfather in the same month. We both had suffered a lost, and as fate would have it, we were being brought together.

Finally there was someone who truly loved me for who I was. I didn't have to worry about living up to Earley's father's expectations or wondering whom she would show up with at the games. I knew I didn't have what it took to compete for Lena, because she wanted more than I could give her. Love, kindness and sincerity were not enough for Lena. She wanted those things and the entire world. All I had to give was my heart and all the love inside, but she wanted the pleasures of this world, and I couldn't afford it. I can say, on Lena's behalf, she never really asked me for anything, but she just seemed to be never satisfied with anything I said or did. I do wonder though if either Earley or Lena honestly knew how I felt.

There were other moments spent with girls, but they seem to come up short when I compare them to the love that Regina had for me. I was beginning to find out that the love of a soul mate is a perfect love, because it is love without fear and it is unconditional. The Bible tells us, "*There is no fear in love; but perfect love casteth out fear: because fear hath torment. He that feareth is not made perfect in love*" (KJV, 1 John 4:18).

Our junior year was the bomb. We started out in football, winning game after game. That was the year we were all in high school together. We still had to pick cotton and chop cotton, and the Nightriders were still in action. Hunting was still the thing we all enjoyed. Sonny had a car and Cleo's dad had bought a truck that we called the Gray Stallion.

Sonny, of course, was younger than us and was always pampered. When we were riding bicycles, put together from miscellaneous parts, he was driving a motorbike. He was driving a car, and we had just escalated from bicycles.

I had an old junk '55 Ford car that didn't run, so we overhauled the engine and added parts. It was a mutt (with all different brands parts) car that we had put together in my auto mechanics class as a project. We called it the Blue Lizard, but it couldn't be driven on the highway. It had no license or registration. The Blue Lizard was what we used to steal watermelons and gas from the farm equipment that was left in the fields at night. If it weren't for the gas taken from the combines, we would have been grounded. It was our transportation to the games, if we took the back roads to get there.

One night we had stolen thirty watermelons from the Man and had stopped next to a well to get some water and to do some watering ourselves. The sheriff came over to where we were, and immediately we brought out a football and started throwing passes to each other in the dark.

All he said was, "Damn, that's why you boys are so good," and advised us to keep up the good work.

I often wondered if that deputy sheriff really believed six Black kids were practicing football at one o'clock in the morning next to a watermelon patch.

I also had a friend name James, and he had polio as a child and was left crippled for life. James and I were very close and I would visit him often. He had a beautiful sister named Jean, but I never got to know her very well. She seemed very distant. He also had a sister named Georgia who I knew well. Georgia was a good friend of my sister Mary, and she belonged to the group of girls who seemed to care about each other.

James could play a guitar extremely well, and we formed a band called

The Hitchhikers. James came to all the games, and I often wished I could get into his mind for a while to see what he thought. I had been there in my childhood, not being able to walk. I empathized with him, because I knew how he felt. I had God to thank for my healing, and I prayed that God would do the same for James. We were running and playing games, and he couldn't even walk. I became very protective of him after seeing one of the Mexican boys hit him in the hallway and attempted to run away. I ran over to help James, who had grabbed the boy before he could get away and would not let go. He was being dragged on the hall floor, and he still would not let go and was trying to fight with his free hand. I ran over to help him and pushed the boy away, insisting that he try doing that with me instead of James. I was so angry that I started for the boy with the intent to kill him, but he ran away. How could anyone attack someone in a wheelchair and think highly of his actions?

I stopped and helped James off the floor and put him back in his wheelchair. He had tears in his eyes, but after I told him how proud I was of him tenaciously holding on to the guy and fighting, the tears disappeared. I kneeled down to his level and we embraced.

I told him, "All right now, when I need help you better wheel that chair over and lend a hand."

We looked each other in the eyes, and he said, "Anytime, bro, me and you together."

There were times when I would go to his house, and we would wrestle on the floor. We would be sitting in the backseat of a car, and we would disagree about something, and the fight was on. He and I would wrestle until someone would tell us to stop because neither of us would give in. One day we got into a serious disagreement, and I made him tie my legs with a rope, and we fought until we both agreed to quit. We were both exhausted and worn out, but neither of us would concede to the other.

Whenever Cleo and I went to games at the University of Arizona, or just went to other places, we would take James, and he loved and respected us for doing it. He was a dear friend and an avid sports fan. His father bought him a car, and James was able to drive it to games and to the Toe to visit us, because he lived in Marana. James gave me a friendship chain, and I wore it with a ring that Shirley had given me. Once I put it on, I never took it off, not even for games. I knew what it felt like to not be able to walk, and I think my empathy kept us connected.

That year we had won most of our games, and the state playoffs were upon us. We were playing against Parker High School, and they were from the Indian reservation. They had Indian kids who weighed over three hundred pounds. When they got off their bus they looked like a team from the prison. Before the game, they came to our side of the field and lined up in front of us, covering the length of the field.

They started doing jumping jacks and saying, "We want Ma-ra-na, we want Ma-ra-na."

They were in total unison with their cadence. I must give it to them; they were an intimidating sight, especially with the three hundred pounders staring you in the face as they did their calisthenics.

Frank yelled to them, "In just a few minutes you're going to get us, chief!"

I told Frank, "Boy, shut up, we don't want to piss them off. The last thing I want to do is piss off a three-hundred-pound Indian wearing war paint."

The players were fired up over this, but they won the toss and we kicked off to them. The battle was on, and we didn't let up on them; in fact, we piled it on. When their school arrived it was in the first quarter. Their cheerleaders and fans ran to the field cheering and screaming, "Go team go," until they saw the scoreboard. It was still the first quarter, and we were leading them twenty-four to nothing. We had caused them to fumble and we scored. We ran back a punt and scored, and we had intercepted a pass, which also resulted in a score. We were yet to go on offense and we were up by three touchdowns and a field goal.

The coach took out the first team, and we sat on the bench most of the game. At the end of the game we were winning by a score of forty-eight to nothing when the coach put in the first team and told us, "Whatever you do, don't score!"

He put the backs on the line and the linemen in the backfield and gave them a chance to run the ball. This was a big mistake because you don't give a lineman the ball and tell him not to score. That would be like giving Frank a pack of bubble gum and telling him not to chew it, or taking Cleo into a toy store and telling him not to steal anything, or telling Leroy not to do something stupid.

We had gotten down to what was the last play of the game, and it was about a minute left. The coach sent in the word, "Don't score!"

Richard told the three backs to line up ten yards behind the other and lateral the ball backwards until it got to the last person. Then we were to play keep-away until the game ended. We did this for twenty-five seconds then, somehow, Carl, who was a lineman, got the ball and headed for the goal line. He wouldn't lateral the ball, and we knew what he had on his mind. Both teams (ours and theirs) tackled Carl on the one-yard line to keep him from scoring.

This resulted in the longest play in school history, which lasted almost thirty-five seconds. We lined up behind the quarterback Richard, who was five yards behind the center; I was ten yards behind him, Cleo was ten yards behind me, and Leroy was almost twenty yards behind him. Each person held the ball until a member of the opposing team approached him, and then he would lateral it back to the next person and block the opposing player. We played keep-away for thirty-five seconds until the gun shot ended the fourth quarter.

The second team backs and receivers had scored more than we did, and the final score was forty-eight to nothing.

My sister Lou was one of my biggest fans, and she was out there hugging me and crying tears of victory. We embraced and were knocked to the ground by other fans who rushed out to greet the players. The community of Marana and Rillito ran unto the field celebrating and squashed us all as we lay beneath the pile on the ground.

Eventually I was able to get up without serious injuries, and as I looked towards the stands, I saw two familiar faces. James was there leaning against the fence on his crutches, and I went over to him and shook his hand and embraced him. The other face was Mama. She had come to see me play.

Now let me explain why this was such a blessing to me. My mother and the other mothers of Rillito were involved in the church and the church was very strict about sports, dancing, music, and even watching TV, although most of us watched what few channels were available. My father had bought a television before he died and we were able to watch TV. My mother and the other mothers of the Toe had allowed us to play sports, which was against the will of some church members.

Frank's mother and my mother supported us. When we sung in our group called The Hitchhikers, both our parents came to hear us sing at the school function. When I saw my mom at the game I ran to her and embraced her, thanking her for being there. She told me to go back with the team and celebrate, and I did.

Before I loosed my embrace, I told her, "Mama, thank you."

She said, "I wouldn't have missed this for the world."

Mama said, "Any rule that tells you not to support your children, well, there has got to be something wrong with it."

My mother never stopped supporting me, and I knew she wanted the best for me. She was the one who directed me toward education and sports, knowing that one day it would provide for me what she could not.

After the game I missed Shirl, and I wanted to share this with her. Frank, Sonny and I went to town to visit the girls and celebrate our victory. Man, it was great. We had won the state title and I was with a girl who loved me as much as my mother did. One thing I do know, it's good to be loved. I wanted to hold on to her because she was real, and her love for me was real. I thought about the scripture that says, "*Let love be without dissimulation. Abhor that which is evil; cleave to that which is good*" (KJV, Roman 12:9).

The following Monday we started basketball practice. It was always like that, from one sport to another. It didn't take long for the transition and we were soon kicking butt. Game after game, Leroy was shooting the eye out of a gnat, but we were not a one-man team. We all contributed to the success of our team.

One day Cleo and I were running to our FFA class because the late bell was ringing. We had to go past the principal's office to get to class, and he stepped out just as we were about to enter the classroom. He yelled our names and called us to his office. He suspended us from the FFA activity dance that weekend. Floyd was the only Black who was allowed in the dance, and that fool went. I guess you couldn't blame him, he hadn't done anything wrong.

We decided to go hunting that weekend; by now, we all had rifles and shotguns. I was an excellent shot because there were times when we had nothing to eat, and Mama would hand me dad's shotgun and a couple of shells and tell me to "go get supper!" I had to make every shot count so I would wait until I saw two rabbits at the same time, and didn't fire until they crossed paths. I would shoot and get both at the same time. I did the same thing for quail and sometimes some of the Man's chickens when I caught them in the desert.

That week the FFA teacher had told us that since we were not allowed to come to the dance, if we came afterwards he would make sure that we got the refreshments that were leftover. So, we decided to go there after hunting and we put the guns in the trunk of the Blue Lizard. We were in the parking lot talking when the principal showed up and started threatening to throw us all out of school. We tried to tell him the FFA teacher had invited us for refreshments, but he didn't want to hear anything these little Black kids had to say. He grabbed both Frank and Lee by the collar and almost pushed them to the ground.

I thought, *Oh my God, I'm looking at a dead man walking!*

Frank had tears in his eyes, and after he escaped the grasp of the principal, he started running directly to the trunk of the car. I knew Frank was going for the gun so he could kill him. I didn't say a word. I ran as fast as I could to head him off, but it was too late. Frank had gotten the rifle out of the trunk and was walking towards the principal, aiming the gun at his head. The principal was now terrified after seeing the mess he had gotten himself into.

I yelled, "Frank! NO! NO!"

I leaped towards Frank and grabbed the gun. I wrestled him to the ground and took the gun. I thought, *Thank God it's over!* Then Lee grabbed a gun, and he was crying and going towards the principal, aiming at his head.

I started yelling, "Stop him! Stop him!"

The others had to take the gun from Lee. The principal was now realizing he could have died twice, and was about to have a heart attack.

He pleaded, "If you boys leave I won't say anything and what happened will be kept to ourselves."

He pleaded and said he was sorry and was glad that we took the guns away before someone got hurt. I should have known that you never accept a promise made out of fear. We drove home from the school that night wondering whose side God was on, the principal's for keeping him alive, or ours for not allowing us to shoot him? Frank was still angry and said he didn't trust the principal.

He said, "That White man is going to turn on us, you wait and see."

On Monday the principal requested that all the Black males to come to his office, except Floyd. Some of the guys who weren't there that night had no idea what was going on. But, if you were a Black male, you had your name called over the intercom, and you were to respond to his office.

When we got to the principal's office, he shouted fervently, "You boys don't have your guns now, let's see how bad you are."

I said, "Sir, I thought you said this was over? I told you the other night we were hunting rabbits and decided to come and get the refreshments that the teacher had promised. It was ten o'clock at night and we were in a public parking lot waiting to talk to the FFA teacher and see what refreshments were leftover from the dance."

He told me to shut up and threatened to kick all the Black players off the team, even the ones who weren't involved. Perhaps he thought we all looked alike. He called the coach to the office, and told him he had better keep an eye on us or he would lose his entire team. He was given the responsibility of reprimanding us, as if it was his fault for having Black players.

The coach took us to the gym and told us to practice for the upcoming game. We told him what happened that night, and he believed us. We told our coach why we were waiting in the parking lot when the principal came over to us and started grabbing Frank and Lee and threatened us. The coach accepted our story as the gospel and had someone keep watch for the principal as we practiced. He was supposed to be reprimanding us for our bad deed, but instead he allowed us to get in some extra practice.

Before the principal would come into the gym to witness our punishment, the coach would have us sit down, and he would verbally reprimand us until the principal left, then we returned to practicing again. This continued for a week and we used the extra practice to demolish the team we played next.

Frank held on to his belief that the principal turned on us, because he was White and we were Black, but I pointed out to Frank that the coaches were White, and they didn't turn on us. I did believe Frank about the principal, and we all knew if it weren't for sports, he would have been satisfied with an all-White school.

We saw a visiting schedule once at another school that predicted the games their team would win or lose, but when it got to Marana, instead of writing win or lose, someone wrote in big letters "PRAY!"

Our next game was in Benson. The day of the game DJ showed up with this small bottle filled with who-knows-what. DJ told us it was a magic potion that would guarantee anyone who drank it would score a lot of points. We all laughed because DJ would only score five or six points a game on the JV team. DJ had us all watching as he drank his magic potion before the game. We had determined there was no way we would put our lips on that bottle, and we certainly weren't going to drink any secret potion DJ had made. For all we knew, our penis could fall off, or we could have turned into White people, or we could become Mexicans.

DJ consumed his secret from the bottle, and we waited for him to start turning into a vampire or werewolf. When he drank the potion, nothing happened. He smacked his lips a couple of times and said, "Hummm good." He still looked the same, so we figured it hadn't kicked in yet.

When DJ started playing, it was as if everybody was in slow motion, and he was the only person going in regular speed. It was incredible. This boy went out there and scored thirty-three points. Man, everybody was asking DJ for some of his magic potion, but he said he drank it all, and couldn't make any more because he forgot what he put in it.

I don't know what DJ put in that bottle. If he could have remembered the ingredients, we could have sold it and become rich, or spent the rest of our lives in prison. He said he could never remember and went back to scoring five or six points a game throughout the rest of the season. Leroy said he thought DJ had beer in the little bottle, but we couldn't tell because none of us knew what beer tasted like except Carl, and he never tasted DJ's potion. I really don't think an ounce of beer caused DJ to score thirty-three points.

Frank and I didn't have a car, with the exception of the Blue Lizard that was illegal on the road, but Sonny did. He was younger than all of us and he had the car. He was blessed, and the boy didn't know it. There were times he would take off and leave Frank and me, but when he needed gas money he would ask us if we wanted to go into town. When Frank and I got to see our girls, they would tell us that Sonny had told them he pleaded with us, but we both refused to go with him.

Shirl's brothers and sisters would ask, "How come Sonny comes up but y'all don't?"

One day it was their mom's birthday and Sonny had dropped us off and gone somewhere. When he returned, he had a gift for their mother for her birthday.

The children shouted, "Why don't you and Frank buy Mama a gift like Sonny does?"

Frank and I had no idea it was her birthday. We pleaded with Sonny, "Let us pay you our share, and just tell her it's from all of us."

No, not Sonny, he walked up there so proud and arrogant and presented his token.

"This is from me," he said to her. "I don't know what Frank and Lacey brought, but I want you to have this as a token of my love."

It was sickening. Frank and I were left standing there with nothing but an overwhelming desire to vomit. Sonny knew it was her birthday, but wouldn't tell us. We hadn't even been to town in two weeks.

On the way home we gave him all the money we had left for gas, and we had nothing left for food. Sonny bought himself some food with some of the money we gave him for gas and ate it in front of us without even caring. When I asked him if he would share his food, he emphatically replied "NO," then suggested that since I was writing in my diary, I should record him telling us no (it is recorded in my diary).

This attitude carried over and became a part of his character. He would expect love and mercy from you, but was the last person to give it out. We all shared, but with Sonny you had to pay him for what he did for you. When he wanted something from you he expected you to give it to him out of loving kindness. He was vain, very insensitive and was often without grace. He hadn't lived in the Toe as long as the rest of us, and what we thought would inevitably change, never did. It was apparent that Sonny was indeed a spoiled, arrogant, self-centered, egotistical, narcissistic brat. Other than that, I was forced to love him through the kinfolk rule.

It would seem that whenever there was a conflict or disagreement about a decision in the games we played, Sonny was always the one to disagree. Clevie Lee would argue with him until the sun went down and came up again. Lee would just walk up to him, and the fight was on. Frank sometimes would fight, and other times he just ignored him and did what he thought to be the right thing. Me, I loved him as a brother and defended him when he was right, and made excuses for him when he was wrong. I don't think Sonny can even comprehend all the times he offended me, yet I took it. I defended him and stood up for him in his presence and his absence.

My mother would always tell me, "That's your cousin, so you take care of him."

I wonder if she ever realized the dynamics of that request. Sonny never had a clue about how abrasive his personality was, and the dissonance he caused. I guess a proud person can never see his true self, but to others he is as transparent as clear glass.

I remember one time when I went to pick up Shirl for a date and Sonny wasn't there. Frank was with me, and during the night Frank and Debbie got very quiet, so I turned and saw them kissing. I immediately took Shirl and Debbie home and had a little talk with Frank about friendship and loyalty. Frank was almost in tears from my verbal lashing, and promised it would never happen again. I don't ever recall that it did.

A day later I went over to Sonny's and he had a .22 rifle, and said he was going to shoot Frank. Apparently Debbie told him that Frank had forced himself on her, and she made Frank out to be the monster. I talked him out of the confrontation and told him that it took two people to do what they did that night. It appeared to me that the kissing was mutual. I was driving and Shirl was in the front seat with me, and I never once heard either Frank or Debbie say "no" or "stop." I knew Frank was wrong, but I also knew Sonny and he would hold this against Frank for the rest of his life. Frank was wrong for kissing her. Debbie was wrong for letting it happen and then blaming Frank.

From that day forward there was always a dissonance between Frank and Sonny. I think Frank totally forgot about what happened, but Sonny never did. I think Debbie was flattering herself by telling Sonny.

They were all my brothers, and in their own unique way, they were all very special people. I knew Sonny's selfishness, arrogance and egotism would take him to high places, but when the memories of all these things subside and are forgotten, all we have is who we are. It is important to stand tall and honorable before your true friends and hold loyalty to the highest esteem. When your fame is gone and time takes away your youth, it is the companion of true friends that makes life worth living.

Frank, Sonny and I were all connected within our natural families. The people in the Toe were also all connected in some way. Everybody was related to each other in some way. That was why it would be dangerous to marry someone from the Toe. You could be committing incest and not even know it. In spite of Sonny's escapades, we fell in love with two sisters and Frank fell in love with their cousin. I often wondered if Frank and Sonny had the right person. I think they should have switched girlfriends and they would have had a more compatible match. I think Frank and Debbie would have been a lifetime match, and Sonny and Mona would have spent their lives fighting for selfish and vain supremacy.

One day Regina (Shirley) told me she preferred to be called Shirl, because Regina was her middle name. She told me she hated the name Regina because it spelled "a niger" backwards. I guess in German niger is the same as nigger. From that moment I started calling her Shirl.

We were all growing up and relationships were developing. Earley was dating Carl because he had a car, or because he took dating to a higher level than I did. Carl was indeed sexually active and sex was something the rest of us just thought about. I do believe there was a degree of innocence endowed in Earley that was void in Lena. Lena was dating boys in Tucson like always, not knowing that the ones who truly cared for her were right under her nose. Perhaps Lena grew up a bit faster than us boys, and may have perceived us boys as being bit immature, so she went with older boys.

I know also that Cleo cared for Lena as a sister, but I never knew if Cleo's feelings ever crossed the line. I suspected it from time to time, because we talked of her often.

I still remember the night we picked her up from home to take her to a game we had that night. She came out dressed in her cheerleader outfit and forgot something and went back into the house to retrieve it.

I remember Cleo saying to me in total astonishment, "Lace, Lena is a girl!"

We saw her for the first time as a young lady and not just our childhood buddy. What a makeover, and we both almost went into shock. We wouldn't dare look at her, because we thought she would catch us staring at her legs that were partially covered by the flimsy skirt or the low-cut cheerleader blouse that accentuated her breasts. The cheerleading uniform heightened every curve of her body, and I think we both went through a cycle of puberty within a few minutes.

Lena was always beautiful on the outside, but on the inside her inner beauty often fell short. Maybe only with me was she very inconsistent; perhaps with others she was different. She may have been a beautiful person on the inside to the boys in Tucson, but not to me. She was still young and growing, and I prayed that one day the inside would catch up to the outside.

Things started happening fast in the Toe. The airmen from town started coming down and marrying the girls, and the Toe Boys started going to town looking for girls. I knew that Carl was not for Earley. Her naivety and innocence could easily be exploited by one such as Carl. I knew Carl was older than us by one year or two, and he was after one thing. I don't know if he ever got what he was after, but Earley was playing with fire. It is written, "*Can a man take fire in his bosom, and his clothes not be burned? Can one go upon hot coals, and his feet not be burned?*" (KJV, Proverbs 6:27-28). That scripture was applicable to Earley courting Carl. I didn't feel that Earley could be in a relationship with Carl and not be burned.

I also believed that one day if Lena wasn't careful, she would marry someone for all the wrong reasons, and her marriage would probably become a nightmare. I knew that somewhere down the line there was a disaster waiting for her.

Basketball ended with us winning the conference again. We had mounted up with wings of eagles and had soared to the highest peak. We had so many medals and letters on our jackets and sweaters that the reflection could blind you. Leroy looked like a four-star general whenever he wore his letterman's sweater or jacket. He had so many medals and honors on it that it must have added ten pounds to the weight of it. I do know that every metal Leroy had on his jacket or sweater represented a moment of success, and was well-deserved.

This was the year that we realized how prejudiced and bigoted some of the baseball coaches really were. The first thing we noticed was the equipment manager gave all the Black players the worst equipment. We were playing both track and baseball up to this point, but that year every Black player quit the baseball team and concentrated on track. Before we left I had gotten a hit every time at bat, but that was not enough to keep me in a situation of bondage.

Richard and I hit home runs at Wilcox High School. I had come up to bat and their pitcher was fast as lightning. The first two pitches I never saw, I just heard the ball hit the catcher's mitt. I had a two balls and no strikes count against me. I decided this boy was very confident with his fastball so he was going to throw a strike. The pitcher wound up and as he released the ball I knew it was blazing in at "warp five" speed. I actually shut my eyes and swung as hard and as level as I could. When I heard the crack of my bat I knew that ball was gone. Sure enough, when I opened my eyes it was over the fence, the highway and still going.

It was then Richard's time at bat, and he did the same thing. I think maybe Richard could have hit another one, but me, I don't think so. Both of our bats put fear in the heart of the coach and the pitcher. After that, the pitcher walked us both every time we came up to bat, but we won the game. I had a perfect at bat, but apparently that was not good enough for the coaches and the Mexican players.

The Mexicans all played baseball and none of them ran track, so to get away from the bigotry and the racism we all went to track. All the Black players walked away from the baseball field over to the track field. We took off our cleats and put on the spikes. We left the shoes right next to the field for the baseball coach and his racist players. There were no problems in track because our basketball coach was the track coach. He cared more for us than some parents.

Richard stayed in baseball and was the best thing they ever had. Richard could deal with the Mexicans, and he never let their attitudes get to him. Whenever we had a chance we would go watch Richard pitch, and he would come to our track meets and watch us run. Man, he was awesome. Little did we know one day Richard Hinton would play for the Yankees.

Track was fun and we were timed individually. We compared our times and found out that we probably had the fastest backfield in Arizona and possibly the nation at that time. The three starters in the football backfield ran the hundred-yard dash in less than ten seconds, and Richard, who was playing baseball, had been clocked at ten seconds flat in the hundred-yard dash. That made him the slowest person in the backfield, but among the fastest on the team.

We were told that this was the year that Leroy would get beat. There was a boy named Beebe from another school who thought he could beat Leroy. Well, the time came for him to show his stuff. The stands were full and the challenge was on. Beebe had to put up or shut up, and Leroy was about to make him shut up. Watching Leroy run was like watching a gazelle with the speed of a cheetah, or like watching a jet airplane climb into the sky. When he ran it appeared so effortless, yet his speed was awesome.

We prepared ourselves in the starting blocks and waited for the gun to sound. A field of eight runners had lined up to do battle. We were set in the blocks, trembling until the gun shot, and we all unwound like a spring. Except for Morris, he exploded out of the blocks like a cannonball in front of everybody. This was normal for Morris up to about thirty yards. He then started tightening up like a tetherball wrapping around a pole, and the rope kept getting shorter until it couldn't go any farther.

Morris was thirty yards ahead of us as we left the blocks. At forty yards, Leroy, Beebe and I had passed him. I think for thirty yards Morris was the fastest human being in the world. I was running neck and neck with Beebe and Leroy was ahead of us about to kick it in gear. Leroy was about five yards ahead of us when he hit the tape, then Beebe and me. To tell the truth, I almost beat Beebe myself, but Leroy was undisputed. That day Leroy was clocked at 9.6 seconds in the hundred-yard dash. I broke ten flat and Beebe was somewhere in between. Like always, Leroy just ran fast enough to win. We never really knew how fast he really was, because he won every race and was never really challenged.

Cleo dominated the hurdles, Frank won the pole fault and we all ran in the relays and won. The rest of the guys took up the slack in the field events and other races. We were ready for the upcoming state meet.

Only the best in the state were to go to the Luke Greenway Track Invitational. Leroy was to be in the hundred and the two-hundred-and-twenty-yard dash. Our eight-hundred-and-eighty-yard relay team had qualified as well. Leroy won both his races and the relay team came in second in the state. We came home with trophies, and the Toe celebrated.

That summer our basketball/track coach took some of the Toe Boys to Pinetop, Arizona, to do some clean up around a cabin that he owned. Mrs. Opal, Lena's mom, worked for our coach, who had a cabin in the mountains, and Cleo, Paul and I went to help out. It was so beautiful, and there were trees that touched the clouds and everything was so green. Moisture fell from the sky, and it wasn't raining. It was much different from the desert. The temperature was much cooler, and we had the time of our lives. We actually played in the snow, which was not endemic to the desert area.

We found a place where the kids hung out. It was called the Dew Drop Inn. We saw what we thought were the most gorgeous girls in the world. I was totally speechless and in awe of their beauty. We went to the house of a friend we had met in sports from McNairy, and he took us to his cousins' house. When he introduced us to his family, for a moment I thought I was seeing angels. One of the girls was named Pauline, and I never forgot her face. I believe at that time in my life I had seen some beautiful girls, but none of them had the physical beauty of Pauline. She had a beautiful complexion, long black hair and a smile that lit up the world. Her sisters were just as lovely.

When we got home I wrote to her, letting her know how beautiful I thought she was. Fate would have it that we would never meet again during high school, but to think that someone that beautiful could even consider me, I was elated. She was an excellent pen pal for a while and wrote love letters that were nothing more than ink on paper, because we would never meet again.

One day Floyd and Lloyd (twin brothers) had asked Cleo and me to go up with them back to McNairy where the girls were. Floyd (who had peed on Cleo) had met one of the girls named Galey at a track meet and had written her letters. I was ready to go and thought I would finally get to see Pauline again, but Lloyd came over and told me in a nice way that I couldn't go with them. Floyd had found out that Pauline and I were writing each other, and he was just being his evil self.

I later heard that Floyd had gone up and fallen head over heels for her sister and while there did his normal detriment, spreading lies. Cleo told me that Pauline had asked about me and had said a lot of good things about me. Pauline and I continued to write for quite some time, but eventually the letters stopped. The spark never got any bigger, and I never pursued it with any enthusiasm.

I was quite fed up with some of the things that had come from Floyd's house, and the detriment caused by saying that none of us would ever amount to anything and denigrating the Toe Boys. I had made up in my mind somebody would die.

Cleo and I were together when Floyd's father was walking by our house on his way to the store. I reached in the corner and loaded Dad's shotgun and was waiting for him to pass by my window so I could pull the trigger. Cleo was pleading with me not to do it, but I had lost all sense of awareness and values. I pulled back the hammer and just as he came into view I pulled the trigger. Cleo grabbed the gun at the same time the hammer came crashing down. The hammer tore the skin between his thumb and index finger. While Cleo and I was wrestling for possession of the weapon, I saw that his hand was bleeding and blood was all over his shirt. I let him have the gun, wondering why it hadn't shot. After Cleo had calmed me down, we examined the shotgun and between the hammer and the firing pin was a piece of Cleo's skin preventing the gun from firing. The flesh torn from his hand prevented the gun from going off. I was in tears, but eventually I came to myself, and I thanked God that he allowed Cleo to be with me that day, because if things were different I could have gone to prison for the rest of my life.

I don't think that man ever knew how close he came to dying. God was on both our sides, and I believe he was preserving me for my calling later in life. Cleo was the instrument of my redemption and prevented what could have been a great tragedy in my life.

There was great sadness when Lena and Syl's family decided to leave the Toe. I remember the thing that hurt me most of all was they never said goodbye. They were like my brother and sister and a piece of me went with them. Their parents appeared to be the perfect match, but I guess looks can be deceiving. You never know what is going on in people's lives until it's too late. Syl was a friend, and Lena, she was more than a friend. We may have had our differences, but I don't think she had a clue as to how much I loved her. She started out like a sister, and then I saw her as a young lady who caused my heart to cross the forbidden zone. I remember the guys making fun of her and calling her Madame Mazelle, and she hated it. I never had the chance to apologize to her for calling her that name. I had seen her at the bus stop, and she was telling everyone goodbye, but she never came to me. I didn't know that I would never see her again. If I had known, there is no doubt in my mind I would have confessed my feelings. It's so easy to say I love you when you're all alone, but I know the thought of never seeing her again would have brought those words out of me. Cleo and I both talked about her to great length, and we worried about where she was, what she was doing and whom she was with. We have always thought of her as a friend.

I wonder what would happen in life if people really knew how certain people felt about them. There would be many changes in the lives of individuals and perhaps changes in our family tree. I guess if we could tell if someone loved us, it could prove to be a disadvantage to love someone with a cold heart or no heart at all. Think of all the people in this world whose lives would have changed, if only they knew that the other person loved them. They would have done so many things different and perhaps they would have married different people.

I wrote a poem once and called it, "The girl of my dreams." It was about the picture or the image we have of a person sealed in our minds. I kept that picture of Lena in my mind. I thought if I had the opportunity to see her years from now, would I really want to see her? I thought to see that person after so many years could change your image of them from being the girl of your dreams to becoming a nightmare.

I never really wanted that childhood picture I had of Lena to be replaced, but I knew that one day perhaps as an adult I would see her, and the images would disappear and be replaced with the current reality. Would she still be distant concerning me or would she disclose to me some pleasant secrets?

The more time I spent with Shirl, the less I thought about anyone else. We were now in a steady relationship and she was becoming more to me than any of the others. I was still determined that not even Shirl was going to stop me from pursuing my education. I wasn't trying to get out of the Toe to get away from poverty. Actually, I never thought we were poor. It wouldn't be until years later that I would look back on my life and realize we were poor.

I was so comfortable around Shirl and she made me feel like a man and not a mouse. I never once thought I was competing with anyone for her love. I wanted to be around my Toe family, and she seemed to want to get away from her family, so it worked out.

My senior year was upon me, and during the summer, instead of working in the fields, I got a job at the school doing maintenance. My ex-principal, Mr. Adams, had came to my house and offered me a job at the school. Mr. Hawkins, one of the coaches, was always giving me clothes, and God knows I needed them.

Cleo and I worked together with big foot Len, who was now a custodian. It sure beat the cotton fields and all them other fields. We cleaned the classrooms and cut the lawn around the school. It was the first time I thought work could be fun. After work, I would train beyond the limit, because I wanted to be in the best condition of my life when the season started. I had gotten that work ethic from Paul, who was now in college. I thought, *If Paul can go to college, I can too.* He had inspired me to rise above circumstances, believe in myself and reach for the stars. My mother added to that by teaching me to believe that with God all things are possible, and the Lord willing, I could climb the summit of any mountain.

CHAPTER SIXTEEN

She Is the One

We were sustained by Social Security checks and commodity food. The Social Security checks were because my dad had been in the military. The commodity food came because Mom was taking care of Frankie and Chris.

One day, I was inspired by my grandmother. My maternal grandmother, Margie (Jackson) Campbell, called me over when she was visiting with us and gave me a dollar bill. She told me that one day I would go to college, and she wanted to be the first to give me money towards my education. She had prophesied to me, and little did I know, one day I would attend college.

During the summer I had two jobs. One job was driving combines for the Man. A combine is a piece of machine used for harvesting. In this case we were harvesting barley and grain. The boss was a Mormon who wore red underwear. I was not one to talk about someone's religion, but to think a pair of underwear can save you is a bit much. I guess if you believe in something so strong, you will give that thing the credit for everything. He had a lot of stories about how his red underwear saved his life.

It is strange how people can put faith in material things and put their trust in those things for their deliverance. It reminded me of the guys in sports who refused to wash their socks for a season, or the guy who hit his head against the locker seven times before each game for good luck. I never believed in luck, I just figured God was in control of everything and sometimes he allowed things to happen and sometimes he didn't. There is a scripture in the Bible that tells us, "*...For he maketh his sun to rise on the evil and on the good, and sendeth rain on the just and on the unjust*" (KJV, Matthew 5:45). We often bring things upon ourselves and God allows us to deal with the consequences. We can either ask for his help or be obstinate and go it alone.

We had been treated with such prejudice by our Mormon boss that I had enough and quit. I went to pick up my last paycheck, and the boss gave me the runaround. He may have worn red underwear during the day, but he gave you the impression that he wore a white sheet over him at night. I think my self-confidence and assertiveness were out of place with him.

Huey worked for him as well, and he never had any trouble with him. By this time Huey had dropped out of school, and this was his livelihood. It became pertinent to his survival to say, "Yessa" and "Nossa." I had no problem with respecting anyone who respected me. If you didn't, I didn't mind letting you know that I was neither a field nigger nor a house nigger. I am a human being! I am a man! I let him know that after he had called us niggers and suggested our intelligence was limited.

I got the Nightriders together, and we went to the field to see the Man. We did some target shooting near the field and immediately he came over and wrote me a check and we left.

I could never figure why White people seemed to bring out the worst in us. If you weren't assertive or even aggressive, they would literally walk over you. I was at that age where I was refusing to be walked on like a carpet on a floor. My days of "yessa boss" and "nossa boss" were over. That was the only job in my life that I walked away from. He told Huey that he fired me, but the truth is I quit. I hated the idea of being called "niggra" and "boy" every time we communicated. Huey stayed with him for the rest of the summer, but even Huey could only take so much, and he quit also.

That summer, Shirl and I got closer together. I realized that she was indeed more than a friend and our relationship started to blossom. She cared for me and was concerned about the little things. If I got hurt she would pamper me, and if there was something bothering me she was there to talk. She cared more for me than I cared for myself. I thought she was a nice-looking girl, but it wasn't until her inner beauty was manifested that her outer beauty shown forth like rays of sunlight on a summer's morning.

I thank God that he showed me her radiance. Getting to know Shirl was like being inside the unopened petals of a beautiful flower and seeing the potential beauty of what was to be. God showed me this beautiful flower before the petals opened to full blossom. I loved her dearly and her tender touch would cause my heart to yearn in her absence. She became my sunshine on a cloudy day, my peace in the midst of the storm and the reason for my every triumph. She was the person who I wanted to be with for the rest of my life.

I knew the union God had caused between us was indeed eternal, a union made in heaven, and I could hear the angels rejoicing whenever we touched. She was a part of my body, my soul and my spirit. My heart was full of love, and I loved her more than anyone or anything, second only to God. I don't know why, but I could not let her know this. I told her that I loved her, but I would always hold back, apprehensive of the memory of past experiences. I think it is a terrible thing to love someone who doesn't love you, and to give of oneself and never to receive true affection in return. I guess bad experiences seem to reside in one's memory for a lifetime.

Shirl was not like the others and everything with her wasn't reciprocal. She would do for me even when I was too selfish or too proud to show my true compassion towards her. Every minute we spent together would be an attack against my defenses, and I knew I couldn't keep them up much longer. With her I was able to see the light at the end the tunnel. I could actually see a glimpse of the future. She was the "substance of things hoped for and the evidence of things I had not seen." I had a goal, a destiny, and it included her. It is written, "*...let everyone of you in particular so love his wife even as himself; and the wife see that she reverence her husband*" (Ephesians 5:33). I did love her very much and she did reverence me.

I knew that one day I would graduate from Marana High School and go to college. I knew that sports were the key, but Shirl was the force or energy to help me turn that key. She was my motivation, and she was my focus and my inspiration, so I prayed and asked God, "If she is the one who you have sanctified for me, then let your will be done in our lives."

It was from that moment on that I realized she was heaven sent, because all good things come from above. I truly believed in my heart that one day I would marry Shirl, and she would be the mother of my children.

I asked, "Is she the one or is there another?"

God said to me, *"SHE IS THE ONE!"*

I knew my mother had been praying for me to find someone who would love me unconditionally, with Agape love, and it happened. My mother's prayers had reached the throne of God.

CHAPTER SEVENTEEN

Three Lucky Punches

My brother had been discharged from the Army and was back home again. I trained with him at the gym, learning to box, and I continued to practice in school athletics. My brother, though he was older than I, was also shorter. I had gotten taller than him but thinner. He was a pretty good boxer who had won several fights and was always trying to prove he was better than me. I really loved my brother Butch and respected what he was doing. He would work twenty-four hours a day and still find time to workout. He was a very stingy person, but would give me a dollar or two every now and then to show off how much he had, and not out of compassion. He didn't have a clue that his niggardly attitude would never allow him great prosperity.

Several times he would send me to the store to buy him a carton of his favorite orange juice. I would poke a hole in the top of the carton with a pin and suck out about one fourth of the juice and then give it to him.

He would get upset and tell me, "Next time shake the carton to make sure I'm getting a full one. Every time you go to the store you come back with a defected carton that isn't full."

I thought to myself, *This boy is dumb!*

He said he didn't believe in Jesus Christ or God, but that Allah was God. Our family was brought up in a Pentecostal church, but my brother never attended. I had been born into the Church of God in Christ. There is a song that says, "You can't join in; you have to be born in." It meant you had to be born again.

Now, my brother was about as religious as a rock. One minute he was a Black Muslim and the next he was a Black Panther. I think he even claimed to be a Jew, and even Hindu. He changed colors like a chameleon. He read about Rap, Huey, Stokey and the others and immediately started pretending he was one of them. Twice we were together when he had a car accident and each time before the collision he would yell out, "Lord, help me!"

He ran into an irrigation ditch once and on the way down I heard him cry out, "Help me, Lord," and when we were rear-ended by another car, he also yelled for God to help him, and another time he yelled, "Jesus!"

Now, me being the curious lad that I am, I asked him, "If you don't believe in God, why are you always asking Him for help?"

His response was, "Actually, I think I missed my calling, because I believe I was supposed to be a preacher."

"If you were supposed to be a preacher," I retorted, "why are you acting like there is no God and then calling him only when you need help? Why is He your God when you are in trouble, but when you are prospering its Mohammed, or Buddha or some made-up name you read about in some book?"

"Just shut up!" he shouted. "And forget it. I don't have to explain myself to a little brat like you."

So I shut up, but intentionally laughed loud enough for him to sense my sarcasm. This was the time when Blacks couldn't decide if they were Black, Negro, African-American or Colored, and whatever they decided had an effect on what God was to them. While my brother was trying to figure out who he was, I had already decided he was stupid and confused.

While traveling to the gym one night, we were rear-ended and it was a minor accident with no injuries. He had cried out, "Help me, Lord" and had apparently gotten through to God, because all was well except that he had allowed me to see a part of him that should have remained a secret. I have learned that people don't like being transparent to others. I often wondered, if God had called him to preach, why was he running? He reminded me of the prophet Jonah, who, when God sent him to Nineveh, went in the opposite direction to Tarsus. I've never forgotten that God prepared a fish to swallow Jonah. I knew somewhere there was a fish being prepared for him. Would he perish in the belly of that fish, or would he be spewed out on the beach, to carry God's word as intended?

We went to training that night and I could sense he wanted to get back at me for my sarcasm in the car. While at the gym they couldn't find a sparring partner for him, so he graciously volunteered me to get beat up or killed. Initially I refused, knowing he only wanted vindication, but the trainer promised me that he would take it easy. Now that was like saying, "I'm going to put some sugar on a picnic table and put up a sign in Spanish telling the ants not to eat it," or God telling the Israelites not to take more manna than they could eat for a day.

Well, they suited me up and I was ready to go through with it. I figured the worst he could do was kill me, and if he did, he would have explain it to Mama. Then she would kill him. Knowing this he would just probably beat me into a coma, which would be a little short of death.

He came after me like a bull enraged over the matador killing his brother. I did all I could to weather the punches, but some got through. I thought to myself, *This is stupid. I know how to box, so why don't I show him a thing or two?* I was taller, faster and almost as strong. Once I got him out of my head, I decided this wasn't going to be a homicide or suicide. If I was going to die that day, I was going to die fighting.

When he came out the next time, I was in the middle of the ring waiting for him.

He saw me make an effort to stand my ground, and grinned and said, "Ahhh, little brother is ready to fight, now show me what you got."

He took a swing at me, and I know if it would have landed I would have gone home headless, but he missed, and I counterpunched him. I threw a three-punch combination starting with a jab, a straight right cross, and then I finished it with a left hook that came from the floor and with all my strength. All three punches landed and he hit the canvas like a sack of rocks. Lou would have envied his fall to the canvas. It was indeed a Kodak moment. It was like in the movies when someone got knocked out. All I could hear was the trainer and the spectators saying in unison, "Oohhh dammnn!"

Now, my mama didn't give birth to no fool, so the first thing I did was get the gloves off and head for the showers before he woke up. I was out of the ring, about to go into the dressing room, when he recovered consciousness. He stood up in the middle of the ring, drowsy and staggering like a drunken man in high heels, trying to keep his footing.

He then yelled, "Come back here, I'm not done with you yet. Come baaack!" POW! He hit the canvas again, still dazed from the punches. They sat him down in the corner and revived him enough to get dressed. I was done and sitting in the car when he got in the car. He made up an excuse and said he had slipped, and I had hit him with a lucky punch.

I laughed and said, "Yeah, three of them."

I knew that for the rest of my life he would seek revenge. I also believe that from that moment I endowed in him a smidgen of fear, which caused some apprehension about messing with me.

I trained hard that year, but I never got to fight. The trainer advised me I would fight in the Golden Gloves tryout in Las Vegas later in the year. Again, I could see that light at the end of the tunnel. I thought, *If I can't go to college maybe I can get rich boxing*, but that was not to be.

CHAPTER EIGHTEEN

A Light at the End of the Tunnel

Football practice was upon us again and it was gruesome. We initially didn't have enough players to scrimmage against a full team. We divided up, and one half of the line scrimmaged against the other. We started practice before school started, but we were asking guys to join the team who we didn't even know. God blessed us and we finally had enough to call ourselves a football team. Our training was twice as hard, we ran three times as far as before, and we hit each other in practice like we were playing a championship game. We had to play both ways—offense and defense—and be on all the special teams.

"No mercy" was the cry, because this was our last year, and we were determined to leave a mark to be remembered. We all had come to the realization that if we, as seniors, were going to college, sports would be the key and our way out of the Toe.

Paul had gone to college and so had Carl. It appeared the sun was setting in the evening of our lives, but in reality, it was still morning.

I prayed, *Please, God, help us to move forward, and please, dear God, don't separate us that we all drift apart, but keep this fire burning within us, this unconditional love that we have for each other and this inseparable compatibility.*

That year we elected Cleo as the captain of the team, but since the captain had to kiss the queen and none of us were White, the school decided to let Richard be a co-captain so he could kiss the White queen during our homecoming game. God forbid one of us kissed that girl in front of all those White folk. They would have shot us before we got out of them funny-looking cars that drive around the field at homecoming. Some of them probably had compressed little white sheets in their back pockets and purses.

My mother told me, "No matter what trials come against you or what names you may be called by scared and ignorant people, keep your head up." She said, "Be proud, because we are more than Black children. We are the children of the Lord. Israel is not lost, we are the spiritual Israel."

I stood up with dignity and told my mother, "Mama, if I am a child of God I must be somebody!"

She smiled, and as the tears filled her eyes, she turned and slowly walked away. I saw her lift her hands up and whisper, "Thank you, Lord."

I knew that it was the prayers of a saved mother who made constant appeals for me before the throne of God that guided and protected me as I went out before the people that year. All of the mothers in the Toe were praying for the children. The boys and girls of the Toe were becoming men and women. The love we received from that little community was worth more than all the silver and gold in the world. We weren't on the mountaintop, but we were high on the hillside and climbing. We weren't completely out of the valley, but we were no longer at the bottom.

We practiced in the rain storms and the monsoons that came upon us late in the summer. The sound of the hitting on that field was like two armored cars colliding. We started the year much the way we had ended it the year before. We were kicking butts and averaging forty points a game. We would get so far ahead of the other team that Coach let the second team play more than the first. Like before, they were scoring more points than the first team players, because they had more playing time.

The older Mexican players had left, and the younger Mexican players didn't know the meaning of racism; in fact, they thought they were Black. We treated each other like brothers. I guess Martin Luther King was getting through. Even Dr. King would have been proud of the unity and the brotherhood of our team.

God took the children of Israel through the wilderness so he could weed out the ones who had an attitude. They were the older ones. Well, I guess you can say that we had come through the wilderness and the older ones had been weeded out. We may have been Black, White, Red or Brown, but we were a team, and our team colors were blue and gold.

It was because of this unity that we became a great team. We had heard the slogan, "I'm Black and I'm proud." Now we were feeling it. But more than that, we had a new cry with no color connotation, "Together we stand and divided we fall." This was indeed a cry without color.

When we went to play games, the coach would stop the bus along the way, and we would get out and line up in formations to test ourselves. On the bus we were constantly going over plays. We all had moved up a level intellectually, but in reference to physical ability Leroy, of course, went up two levels. We were more than a team, we were a family.

Leroy was awesome, and the rest of us gained reputations equally atrocious. Our plays were ingrained into our minds, and every time we ran a play we expected to score. We had such confidence that each of us felt if we got the ball it was a touchdown. Anything less was disappointing. Our coaches were sticklers on basics and fundamentals. We ran the same play until the other team proved they could stop it.

Once, against Flowing Wells High School, we ran the same play nine times in a row. On the tenth time, the defensive player, who had gotten run over nine times before, simply moved out of the way. He threw his helmet on the ground and walked off the field in frustration.

We showed the greatest sportsmanship and every time we would make a block or tear a player apart with an explosive tackle, we would reach down and give them a hand to lift them from the ground.

My father always said, "The only time you should look down on a man is when you're picking him up." I finally understood what Dad was saying, and the gratitude that came from such courtesy and love toward your fellow man.

The next day there was a picture of Frank in the newspaper that read, "A Tiger on the Loose." The players from the other team said we were the hardest-hitting team they had ever played, and the most polite. They said, "After these guys knocked you to the ground, we would look up and there would be a Black hand reaching down to help you up."

We played against Tombstone, Arizona, and the town "too tough to die" got buried. The score was sixty-nine to nothing and Leroy, Cleo and

I saw most of the game from the bench, because they had taken us out as a token of grace and mercy. The coach got upset with Richard, because we needed a yard for a first down and Richard ran a quarterback sneak.

I heard him telling Richard, "You've got three guys in that backfield who run the hundred in nine seconds, and you have the audacity to carry the ball?"

I thought to myself, *Poor Richard.* Actually, coach was only kidding with Richard; I hope he knew that.

Our football coach, Coach Morrison, had a bald head, and he always wore a cap. He loved us like his own children and was determined to get us scholarships. One time in practice, just as he pulled off his cap, Cleo kicked a football that went across the field and hit Coach right on the top of his bald head. We started laughing and we knew Cleo was going to get it.

Coach called Cleo over to him, put his arms around him and said, "Son, you have this whole damn football field. In fact, hell, you have the whole world to kick that ball in, why did you have it land in the spot that I was standing?"

We were laughing so hard because on the top of Coach's head was the shape of half a football.

Coach Hawkins was our line coach. He would go against us without pads, but he did put on a helmet, because one day when Carl was around he challenged Carl and got knocked on his butt. Carl almost sent Coach to the Promised Land, so from that time on he at least put on a helmet. Coach Hawkins later took over the baseball team after all the bigots left and had decent teams. We loved him dearly and there was no sacrifice that he wouldn't make for us.

We were undefeated, and the championship game was coming up. We had our homecoming game and were way ahead at halftime. The halftime festivities were much like we expected. Cleo and Richard stayed for halftime to walk the queen onto the field, but Richard was the one who went to the center of the field and kissed her. I guess many things changed and some stayed the same. Marana wasn't quite ready to erase all biases, but much of the blatant racism was long gone or well hidden. Racism had to disguise itself, and it became more subtle. If you looked hard enough you could still see it. It dressed different and it looked more sophisticated, but it was still there.

We had become a powerhouse and demolished the teams we were playing against, keeping our forty-point average. We were undefeated and still going.

The next week we ventured into a moneymaking scheme that crystalized when Richard kissed the queen at the homecoming. We noticed all the girls who saw Richard kiss the queen seemed to envy the queen. We convinced Richard to get into a phone booth and we sold kisses. He was reluctant, but eventually conceded when we promised him half the money. We charged twenty-five cents a kiss, and we were making money like crazy and Richard was enjoying it. Man, it was White girls lined up inside and outside the building waiting their turn. There were even a couple Black girls in line, and I think maybe a couple of White guys.

Somebody went and told the principal, and he came and took all of our money and threatened to suspend us. We knew that was a lie, because the championship game was yet to come, and Black or White, if you were on the team, there was no way the school was going to risk not going undefeated.

We continued our reign and were undefeated when the championship game came around. We were to play against Wilcox and we knew those corn-fed boys were as much country as we were. They had one Black player on the team, and they were ready to play.

The game was tough and we did all we could, but we just couldn't break away. The score was seven to six and they were winning. Time was running out and Richard had called a play for Leroy to sweep to the left side and I was his blocker. I blocked the defensive end, and he hit the ground, so I maintained my footing and kept going.

I looked behind me and there was Leroy yelling, "Go, Codas, go!"

We had outrun the linemen and there were two defensive backs coming up fast. I thought to myself, *If I take this first guy out, the second has a chance to get Fox*. I met him with all my strength and hit him with such force he laid out before me, and I was still on my feet.

I could feel Leroy tugging at the back of my jersey and yelling, "Go, go!"

The last guy knew he was their last hope, and he lunged forth, attempting to take both of us out at once. I took my forearm and lifted him up. He straightened up and the power of the blow knocked him backward. I ran through him and over him, and then I turned to see if there were players approaching from the rear. Leroy had broken off my block and was headed for the end zone. I knew there was no one in the world who would catch him from behind, but he had slowed down to take advantage of my blocking.

I turned to look and the Marana players had mowed down the defense like grass. I don't think there was an opposing player standing. I turned back to see where Leroy was, and he was crossing the goal line. My heart soared with excitement. Leroy and I both were running towards each other, and as we met, we embraced.

"Leroy, you did it, you did it!" I shouted with exuberance.

"I couldn't have done without you, Codas! I couldn't have done without you!" he replied.

The rest of the team covered us like a blanket, and Leroy and I lay at the bottom of the pack. They all peeled off one by one, but we knew the game wasn't over, because there was still a little time left. We tried the extra point and failed.

Wilcox had gotten down to their last play and it was a tricky one. They had designed a play that appeared as if a player was late getting off the field, but in reality he was a legitimate player, who appeared to be waved off the field by the quarterback, but was going to turn and streak down the sidelines for a Hail Mary pass. When he turned and went down the sidelines, Cleo was on him like white on rice, and as Gootee would say, "stink on do-do"!

The pass was thrown and caught, but Cleo buried his helmet in the guy's chest and laid him out like a flat cotton sack. The ball slowly rolled off the guy's chest because his arms were too limp to grip it.

The gun went off and the game was over. There was a great pile-on in the middle of the field, and Lou, of all people, was there with the players. I don't know how she got there so fast. We all embraced and headed for the coaches. We soaked the coaches with water from the containers and carried them off the field. James was there, and I went over to him like always and shook his hand. The next day the papers read "Marana, State Champions."

That game was played on a Saturday, and on Monday we had a basketball game with Flowing Wells. Man, I think we shot thirty percent from the field and I don't recall how many free throws we missed. I believe our free throw percentage for that game was about twenty percent. Believe it or not, we won the game, because we shot three times as many shots as the other team and got three times as many rebounds. We were in such good shape that we ran those guys into the hardwood. It was pathetic. I would attempt a layup and miss, Cleo would rebound, shoot and miss, then Frank would try to tip it in and miss, and finally Richard or Leroy would accidentally tip it in. The whole game was like that; we had rebound after rebound and took shot after shot.

Coach Carroll sat there just as calm as could be. I guess he realized without any practice we did well. Both the first and second team had played on the football team, and the first time we saw the basketball was when we stepped on the floor to play that night. Coach realized that the transition from football to basketball couldn't come overnight.

After the game, Coach encouraged us to keep our heads up because this was our year. The next few games we continued to win, and the team started to look like a basketball team. All of the racial headaches had left, and we were destined for glory.

Cleo and I were still in FFA and we had the opportunity to castrate, brand and dehorn cattle. We cut boar hogs and helped to deliver piglets. We grew peanuts, cotton, barley, corn and alfalfa for feed. Our FFA teacher, Mr. Despain, was a wonderful person and knew a lot about farming and ranching. He even put in for Cleo and me to receive a scholarship at the end of the year.

Once we were up at the ranch and we had mountain oysters for lunch. We finally found something that Leroy couldn't do. The boy couldn't rope a calf, no matter how hard he tried.

We also worked with Mr. Elliot on his chicken ranch, and ate eggs until every time we had gas it smelled like ammonia. Man, we couldn't even stand our own poots, so we didn't dare have gas in a closed room for fear of suffocating. Mr. and Mrs. Elliot were two people I loved dearly. I had never seen two people so kind and understanding. They gave us a job, and they fed us. We had gone to school with their sons, and they were much like their parents: color-blind.

One thing I do know is those White people sure were good to us. I was beginning to believe that good people do come in all colors. Things were getting better, and I could actually see myself possibly leaving the Toe and seeing the rest of the world. I know it was an impossible dream, but dreams do come true, and the light at the end of the tunnel was getting brighter.

CHAPTER NINETEEN

Disappointment

I was busy working around the house the day of a Saturday basketball game and took a nap. Frank came by and woke me up, and we caught a ride down to the school to catch the bus to go up north to play. When Frank and I got to the school we were told the bus had left earlier. We realized we had gotten our times mixed up. Frank and I tried hard to thumb a ride to the school where the game was to be played, and ended up stranded about thirty miles outside of town. We had no idea how to get to the visiting school because we had never been there before. We were stranded for about six hours. By the end of the day we realized we had blown it and caught a ride back to the Toe.

The next game Coach started someone else in my place and it hurt, but I understood. He didn't have any idea how hard we tried to get to that game, and we had simply misunderstood about the time of departure. I was put in the game in the second quarter and contributed to our win. I accepted my punishment and thc ncxt game I was back in the starting lineup. I thank Coach for that lesson in discipline. I learned that it was still my responsibility to be there on time, and no one could be held accountable for me.

The next game we played was a tight game, and we were down by one point. Leroy and Richard fought for a rebound and snagged the ball off the rim. Immediately I took the outlet pass, and with time running out, I wanted to make sure I wouldn't miss so I drove for a layup. All I could think about was the time running out on me, so I leaped in the air, and as I floated towards the basket I could see the clock showed one second left. It seemed as if I had gone into the twilight zone, because everything seemed totally quiet, and I could hear my heartbeat. I felt my body switching to slow motion as I allowed the ball to roll off my fingers and into the hoop. When my feet hit the ground, my eyes were watching the ball go in. The sound returned, and my body became limp with exhaustion. I could feel arms wrapping around me, forcing me to the ground, and for a moment everything went dark. I thought the other team member was fouling me on the shot, but it was my teammates rejoicing in the victory saying, "We won! We won!"

Everyone was screaming, "We won!"

We knew we were on our way to Phoenix for the championship.

A week later we were on our way to Phoenix, and we were prepared to spend the weekend and play the championship game. The team we were going to play in the first round was Mingus High School. We had beaten them during the season, and they didn't even bring a change of clothes, because they knew they would be going home. We were already thinking about whom we would play for the championship, and poor Mingus didn't make anyone's list of final hopefuls.

When the game started we jumped up by ten points immediately and even increased that to fifteen points during the game. We were up fifteen with about three minutes left in the game. The coach took out the first team, but Mingus left in their starters. We didn't have water bottles so I asked Coach if I could go to the water fountain to get a drink. Cleo, Leroy and I ran to the fountain and on our way we could hear the cheering in the background. Mingus had stolen the ball a couple of times and was now down eleven points. We hurried from the fountain and ran back to the bench, screaming for the second team players to call time-out. It was incredible because the players would not call time-out and neither would the officials recognize our attempts from the sidelines to get their attention. I could not believe my eyes. The second team had gotten so caught up in the game that they paid the coach no attention at all. We yelled for Sonny and Frank to foul someone so the clock would stop, but there was no response. It was now less than a minute and we were only ahead by five. There was total mayhem in the gymnasium. Everyone was on their feet, screaming and stomping their feet on the floor, making the noise decibels rise to record levels. The second team was trying to throw the ball inbounds and again Mingus stole it twice and was now down by one. All I could say was, "Oh my God!" Totally oblivious of everyone trying to give them instructions and yelling for a time-out, they attempted a long pass to the other end, which was intercepted. We were on the court screaming, "Foul the guy, foul the guy," but they wouldn't listen. The Mingus player took the ball and they let him drive the length of the court. I'm thinking, *Tackle him! Do anything, just stop him!* I knew if we could get back in the game we could win.

All our hopes and dreams were destroyed with a layup at the last second of the game. We stood in totally disbelief as we watched the ball go in. I thought, *This must be a dream, this can't have happened.* They beat us by one point. All I could think about was how I could kill the whole second team without going to prison. They were pointing fingers at each other and blaming each other for the loss. I cried for hours and I didn't want to talk to anyone. What a lesson I learned about overconfidence. We were destined to win the state championship, but Mingus had done the impossible. They had upset Marana!

We stayed for the rest of the tournament. Mingus had to go home after the game to get clothes and make arrangements to stay at the tournament. We watched Mingus play the next day. The next game poor Mingus got blown away. Their beating us was a fluke. The team that won the tournament we had beaten twice during the regular season. This was our senior year, and there would never be another season to make up for the loss.

Besides losing that game, the one thing I remember about that weekend was seeing Syl and Lena's dad. He was living in Phoenix now after his separation from his wife and family. We told him that we lost, expecting to be encouraged or consoled, but instead he started laughing. I thought how strange for this man to laugh at us. He used to live in the Toe, but now he looked down on us, and his attitude was very denigrating. He commented that we were a bunch of country boys and could not compete with the kids from the city. Why was he so cold and apathetic? I didn't know at the time why he and his family left the Toe or why he and his wife had separated. I guess for us to come to Phoenix and lose a game was a vicarious victory for him. It appeared that it was some type of vindication for him to hear that we had lost. It was as though the Toe had done something to him, and he rejoiced in our defeat. Was there something wrong in his life that he blamed on us? The mere fact that we were from the Toe seemed to bring out a vindictive nature that I had never before seen. This was indeed one of the greatest disappointments of my life, and it will always be an unforgettable moment.

The following week we were miserable. All we could think about was that after four years of preparation we had failed in becoming the basketball champs.

The only way we could vent our frustration was to go hunting. Everything in the desert knew when something went wrong, because all hell would break loose. At that time in our lives almost everyone had a gun. No more bows and arrows, homemade spears or slingshots. Everybody had a serious weapon. By this time crazy Gootee was in the Navy, so we didn't have to worry about someone lying about who shot what. Gootee, Lloyd and Duck were now the Navy's problem. Vernon (Duck) came home from leave one day and said often he found himself running with his squad. They'd have one hand on their crotches and the other on their weapons. They would sing:

This is my weapon, this is my gun
This is for fighting, and this is for fun

We took the Blue Lizard and went hunting. We took turns letting different people sit on the hood with guns, and they would give a signal for the driver to go to the left, right, or stop. The guys on the hood or fenders would tap on the fender to let us know which side the rabbit was on. Sometimes they would just point and the driver would immediately turn the vehicle in that direction. We were always throwing people off the hood. I thank God no one got shot.

Sometimes the farmer's chickens would hang around the outskirts of the fields, and we would shoot them. DJ said they were wild chickens, and we knew he was lying, but we didn't care.

We found a combine in the field and took enough gas to fill up the Blue Lizard. We thought we would do this one guy a favor that was working at night. We left him a couple of stolen watermelons and took his lunch.

When we realized he had bean sandwiches for lunch, we figured he got the best deal ever.

A few days later, my sister Mary got married and left home. That left me with big Lou, Frankie and Chris. Mary was keeping house and would help Mom with money problems. What were we going to do now? Then Lou said she was planning on getting married, but I knew she was lying, because I once tried to pay a guy to marry her, and he refused the money.

By now Frankie was drinking, smoking cigarettes and soulrettes (marijuana). He was becoming an irresponsible brat, and thought the world owed him a living. Mom continued to cater to his every whim, and poor Chris started looking at him as an example. Frankie would steal stuff and was always trying to make a quick dollar. I trusted him about as far as I could throw a tractor. I would leave change (money) in the ashtray of the Blue Lizard, and Frankie would steal it. One day he even broke the window of the Blue Lizard just to steal a few cents of change. He didn't care whom he stole from, but it seemed that family members were his preference.

Clevie Lee told me he saw Frankie break my car window and commit the criminal damage and the theft. I thought to myself, *Both of these kids (Frankie and Chris) are going to end up in prison for much of their lives if they don't snap out of it.* They had no respect or loyalty for family or themselves.

I knew I had to rise above all my adversities and disappointments in life. I was determined to make it, and I wanted Mama to be proud of me. I could see that Frankie was becoming a lost cause, and Chris was in his shadow.

There were times when I would lay in bed and listen to the rain dripping into the buckets on the floor. The drops of rain would seem to be in harmony as they fell into the buckets containing different levels of water in them. Sometimes it was like a symphony being played out. I went to sleep many nights while listening to a symphony of raindrops.

It was much better than the cabins we once lived in. At least when I looked at the ceiling I couldn't see the stars and the moon through the cracks in the roof, like in the cabins. I remember as a child looking through the cracks in the ceiling and counting the stars. I knew that even now, I could see that God had brought us a long way.

I could have allowed myself to use my adversities in life as an excuse and go in the direction of self-pity or blaming everyone else for my problems, but I refused to do that. Frankie seemed to enjoy having the pity-pat parties, stealing and lying; he grew up expecting handouts.

One day Frankie and Sonny were sent to "Mother Higgins" (juvenile detention) for stealing. He felt the entire world was responsible for him being alive and felt the world owed him a living. Frankie measured his friendship by how much a person was able to give him. He was becoming a parasite and he didn't care whose blood he sucked. He was a person with a welfare mentality and enjoyed it. I don't think there is any such thing as welfare program, it's really the fare-well program, because when you get involved you can say farewell to a normal life.

It was during those times when the rain would fall that I begin to think about my life and what direction I would take. I realized that it was my choice to take the path of good or evil. Mama would say there is a narrow way and a broad way. I took the narrow way, which is called the way of the righteous. This is the road that very few take. It is called in the Bible "the narrow path." It is written: "*Therefore all things whatsoever ye would that men should do to you, do ye even so to them: for this is the law and the prophets. Enter ye in at the strait gate: for wide is the gate, and broad is the way, that leadeth to destruction, and many there be which go in thereat: Because strait is the gate, and narrow is the way, which leadeth unto life, and few there be that find it*" (Matthew 7:1'2-14, KJV).

I prayed that God would make it possible for all of the Toe Boys to have an opportunity to get a higher education, but most of all to keep us in fellowship with one another.

My prayer was "Lord, help us to continue to love each other until the day we die. Keep us in touch, never to forsake one another or to become apathetic towards each other."

I loved the Toe Boys and they loved me, so I knew God would hear and answer my prayer. We seemed to be the last generation of hope, because those after us, like Frankie, Chris and others, were already indulging in drugs and alcohol as well as criminal activities. They had no sense of morals, ethics or values. It seemed that the first ones they would mistreat or use would be their close relatives, then their so-called friends.

Our final season of track was upon us and we were determined not to be overconfident in anything we did. We had learned, by the mistakes we had made in basketball, never to be overconfident in anything. We wanted to be the best, and we pushed each other to the limit. We accepted no excuses for failure, and we encouraged one another to reach for excellence. We started reaching for our dream and we settled for nothing less.

CHAPTER TWENTY

Soul Mate

The children of Israel were kept in bondage in Egypt. I believe everyone has an Egypt in his or her life and they are all trying to get to what they believe to be the Promised Land. We believed that Egypt was our situation and condition, and the Promised Land was some college or university. A place where we could learn and gain the knowledge and understanding that was necessary for a Black child to make it in a White man's world. We knew college was the answer for many of us, but who would be able to go to college and who would be able to escape the call of Uncle Sam? If it really was a war in Vietnam, which of us would go? Would that person ever return? How many Toe Boys would be lost in Vietnam? Those were the questions we had to face, and those were questions of reality.

Cleo and I were elected as co-captains for the track team. Cleo was excellent in the hurdles, both the high and low hurdles. Frank was in the broad jump and the pole vault. Leroy and I ran the sprints and we chipped in on the field events. We all ran in the relays. I didn't mind running the sprints even if I got second place all the time behind Leroy.

Coach placed me in the quarter mile dash during a track meet at Flowing Wells High School, because he needed someone to fill in. Apparently the other team only had one runner in the quarter mile and Coach figured if he put another runner and me in there with Floyd, who was our quarter mile person, we could possibly get three places. We figured Floyd would get first, the runner from the other team would get second and Jerry A. and I would get third and fourth just for finishing the race. Jerry A. was Duck's nephew.

The gun went off and the race was on. Jerry A. and I passed Floyd and the other runner, but we knew it would be short lived, because these guys ran this event constantly and we were just filling in for one day. When I got to the 330-yard mark I decided to kick it in gear for the final hundred and ten yards and Jerry was right behind me. We both figured if the main runners were going to win they would have to catch us to do it. If we gave it all we had, we wouldn't get blown out. I looked ahead and I could see the finish line, but where was Floyd, and where was the other guy?

The Toe Boys were cheering us on, and I could hear Lee yell, "Codas, you got it, you got it!"

I crossed the finish line and turned to see how close Floyd and the other runner were behind me. I saw Jerry A. cross the line totally exhausted, and I heard someone tell him, "You got second." We both crossed the line that day first and second. Floyd and the other guy came in third and fourth. That was my debut and from that day forward Coach had Jerry A. and me running the quarter mile. Poor Floyd never recovered and was moved to the half mile run instead, where he did reasonably well.

Coach Carroll was an inspiration to us. He believed in us more than we believed in ourselves. He was a reserve officer in the Marines and was always neat and professional.

I thought Leroy was getting smarter in his senior year until an argument broke out after he and Frank had run to see which one would be part of the mile relay. Neither one really wanted to run the quarter mile. It was apparent because they gave it less than their best.

Coach Carroll told them that a one-legged man on a motorcycle could have beaten them both. Leroy and Frank argued with the coach about being beaten by a one-legged man on a motorcycle, and the rest of us were falling out laughing over the conversation. Coach, trying very hard to keep a straight face, told Leroy and Frank again that a one-legged man on a motorcycle could beat them around the track. Frank and Leroy was adamant about the fact that no one-legged person could beat them. We kept trying to explain to them that it didn't matter how many legs the guy had it was the motorcycle they were running against. They just couldn't get it, so we let them go ahead arguing about beating a one-legged man on a motorcycle.

We won almost every track meet. Leroy never lost a race; Cleo and Frank were winning the hurdles. I did my thing in the quarter mile and the rest of the Toe Boys were holding their own. I had a problem running the curves, and sometimes it seems that I had to take the turns on one leg. When others saw me run those curves they thought it was funny, but I was doing all I could to stay in the lanes.

We were invited to the Pueblo High School Invitational, and we did our thing. Once again though I had to take the turns on one leg, but I won the race. Our quarter mile relay team was one of the fastest in the country. We were only a class B team, but we were notorious for our speed.

We had our state invitational at the University of Arizona and that was a big thing for us. We were invited in certain events, and we won them all. When it came time for me to run the quarter mile, I realized there was a section of people sitting there just to see me run the curves. Again I didn't disappoint them, for God was on my side, and when God is on your side you will be victorious.

I would visit Shirl after games or track meets, because during the week it was too hectic with practices and all. By now I believed that God had joined us together and "what God has joined together let no man put asunder."

Little did I know that the girls I grew up with were not what God had planned for me. I don't know what my life would have been like if I would have stayed with any of the others, but I do know that God would have disapproved. There were no more feelings for the others. The more time I spent with Shirl the more I loved her and the less I felt for the others. She showed her love for me in so many ways, that to even think of being with anyone else was out of the question.

In retrospect, I thank God for unanswered prayers. I know there really aren't unanswered prayers, just "no" answers from God. I had asked him for the love of people who didn't love me. I had even prayed that God would make them love me, but with Shirl, God did not have to make her love me, she just did. It is good to love someone who loves you even more. I have prayed for so many things in life that would have been detrimental to me. I thank God for answering "NO!"

It seemed that each year Shirl became more beautiful in her appearance and in her behavior and actions. She laughed with me and she cried with me, but most important she was with me in body, mind and in spirit. I saw the way she cared about both our mothers. How she would sacrifice for her brothers and sisters, who never had the slightest clue nor did they ever show any appreciation.

She kept the many secrets surrounding their birth that only a mother would know. Some of her brothers and sisters didn't even know who their fathers were and though she knew, she maintained the secret for her mother's sake. These were actions I highly disagreed with. She even told me she did not believe her given last name was correct. She stated it was very obvious because of the way she was treated. The person whose name she had would treat her other brother and sister with love, but her he neglected. She cried in my arms, telling me that a true father would not treat his child in such a manner. She would learn later in life that she was right. He was not her father and had married her mother when she was pregnant with her. Oh, what a tangled web we weave.

The more we learned about each other the closer we became. Our souls and spirits were touching. She was my soul mate, and it was manifested day by day. There was no doubt, I loved her so very much, and she was the one who I wanted to spend my life with until death would separate us. The feelings I had for Shirl were different than for Lena and Earley. I only wanted acceptance from them, but Shirl was a part of my body and without her I would not be complete.

I believe everyone in this world has a soul mate and you are destined by Divine will to be together. The reason so many marriages don't work is because we are connecting up with people who are not our soul mates. If a person opens their heart and gives God total control, then and only then can one be united with their soul mate.

It is that person you see at random, perhaps at an airport or on the street, and you think you know them. You have this overwhelming longing to talk to them or be with them and when they disappear you get this sick feeling down on the inside. I believe you really do know them and it is your spirit reaching out to his or her spirit, your souls longing to be connected.

When two soul mates meet for the first time, there is a feeling or a sense of recognition. I believe God will allow almost every person to meet his or her soul mate. They will have the opportunity even though they may not take advantage of it. You may have a chance to go to France or to another city or state, and because you follow your intuition you have the chance of a lifetime. That one person who God has chosen for you will be there, so don't reject the opportunity or you both will suffer.

I believe in some cases this missed opportunity can be tragic. When this strong feeling comes upon you take heed and give chase. Take the initiative and don't be afraid to face up to the other person, because they are feeling the same even if they deny it. They are having strange feelings around you, but they don't quite understand why. If they pretend not to be affected by your presence it is because their emotions are somewhere other than where their spirit and soul are. Your heart or emotions can connect you to an eventual nightmare, but your spirit and soul will connect you to your helpmate for a lifetime.

During our senior year we had a couple of athletic scouts come to the school and time us in the hundred-yard dash. We were told that they were very impressed, but we never knew which colleges sent them. Later it was announced that I was to play in the high school all-star game in Flagstaff, Arizona, during the summer. That was some distance away and I was more concerned about the Luke Greenway track meet that came up at the end of the year. This represented the best in Arizona. We were only invited in three events: the hundred meters, the two hundred meters and the four hundred meter relay.

We ran with all our hearts and God was with us. Leroy, Cleo, Frank and I won the relay. It was time for Leroy to run the one hundred and the two hundred meters. We all knew that Leroy always ran fast enough to beat whoever he was running against, but that was in Class B high schools. There he would be running against all classes of schools, including Triple A.

The time had come for all the big schools to put up or shut up. There was no doubt in our minds that Leroy was going to smoke them. We were tired of all the talk that was going around. The other runners were saying that he never had any competition. I thought that was a slap in our faces because we were the ones who pushed him to be the best he could be.

The gun sounded and those boys were tough; after all, they were the fastest in the state. It was a dead heat at about the halfway mark, but you could see the others straining and Leroy hadn't quite kicked it in gear. Leroy tucked his chin in and the after-burners came on. He made it look like everyone else was in slow motion. Leroy was about to vindicate Marana and the Toe Boys. I had never seen Leroy run out of anger, but that day the heavens opened and the force was with him. He began to move away from the pack and soloed through the tape with a record-breaking run. We all ran to congratulate him with multiple embraces.

When he got his medal he lifted it up to us, the Toe Boys, as a toast for victory. We knew that he deserved it, and we were glad to have been witnesses to this great triumph. That day our hearts were with Leroy and once again he was our hero. It seemed that we were all heroes to each other at one time or another. The love and respect we had was immeasurable. The measuring stick that measured our love for each other is kept in heaven and only God knows the numbers. That day we stood tall, and we stood together. We were Toe Boys growing up.

The year was coming to an end and we would all go our separate ways. Leroy, Cleo and I were offered scholarships to go to Arizona Western, and they wanted us to come up and check out the campus. Leroy also had an opportunity to graduate with us by taking the G.E.D. test in Yuma where Arizona Western College was located. We figured we could kill two birds with one stone. Frank had a car by now, and it was an old 1954 black Ford. You had to push it to get it started most of the time, but it got us to where we wanted to go. Frank went with us even though he had another year because he flunked a grade. We drove from Tucson to Yuma with only gas money.

When we got there we were hungry and broke. Now you may think this was a tragic situation, but it wasn't, because we had Cleo. This boy could steal so good he should have been working for the C.I.A. If they needed documents stolen, he could be the perfect Black James Bond.

Cleo would go into the store and come out with all the cold cuts we needed. He really surprised me when he came out one day with items as big as a loaf of bread and a carton of orange juice.

On the second day he decided that he would take me in the store and show me how to steal some meat. We went over to the meat section, and Cleo was calm and cool as he was giving me instructions on how to conceal the meat.

He said, "Take the meat like this, Lace, and open your shirt and put it in like this."

He then showed me his empty hands like a magician does before and after he performed a trick. He then took some cheese and repeated the same thing. I was starting to feel confident, so I took a package of meat.

Cleo was quietly giving instructions, "That's it, Lace, now put it in inside your shirt."

I was shaking so much that I was about to pee on myself, but I kept my composure. I took the meat and was about to put it inside my shirt when I thought I heard a noise. I took the meat and threw it back into the meat section and ran out of the store with Cleo and all the customers staring at me like I had lost my mind. I was so paranoid I thought everyone in the store were undercover agents. I ran out of the store and went past the car. Frank and Leroy started yelling and were trying to get my attention.

I could hear them yelling, "Fool, where you going?"

I was determined to run back to Tucson if necessary and I would have, if Leroy hadn't caught me and led me back to the car. I got in the car and there was Cleo and Frank.

Cleo was angry; he told Frank and Leroy, "Don't ever send this boy in the store to steal nothing. He can steal gas from farm equipment, watermelons and cantaloupes, but the Negro panics if he has to steal a piece of meat from a grocery store."

Later we went to the campus and Leroy took his exam. We hung around for a few more hours then decided to come home. Cleo said he wasn't going to feed us anymore, so we came home and prepared ourselves for the end of school. We still wondered if we would be able to get out of the Toe.

Graduation was coming up and I had nothing to wear and Mama didn't have the money to buy me anything new. Sonny, Frank and I had invited the girls to my graduation, and we were going to a graduation party afterwards. I was about to cancel the date because I didn't have any money either. I knew that Frank and I would have to buy the gas if Sonny was driving. Lou was graduating with me since she had failed the previous year.

I was in tears, and I walked a short distance to be alone and prayed to God that he would work out my problem and bless me to make it through this graduation. I have always been blessed by God to have anything I really need. I realized when I returned home that evening before the graduation that God was smiling on me. It was a shock when my brother Junior drove up from nowhere and handed me some money for graduation. He then told me to go to his car, and there was something he wanted me to see. I went to the car and there, wrapped in clear plastic, was a brand new blue suit. He had bought it just for me and it was the perfect size. It was then that I realized he really did love me as his little brother.

He said, "Yeah, my little brother is gonna be sharp tonight." He then looked at me, trying to hold back tears of joy and said, "Knock 'em dead, Bra!"

I reached out to embrace him and for a brief moment I did, but he was embarrassed of being caught up in such an emotional moment and tried to gather himself by saying, "Okay now, that's enough, just go get 'em, Bra."

That night Cleo and I received an FFA scholarship to be applied to whatever school we attended. I also heard that A.S.C. (soon to be Northern Arizona University) was interested in me.

Leroy had received the results from the G.E.D. test, and he passed. I guess he was always a lot smarter than we gave him credit.

That night we all went out with the girls. Shirl and I went to the graduation party with Frank and Mona. Sonny was his old self, and he and Deborah went by themselves after sneaking away. I knew that this mischievous behavior was all about Sonny, because Deborah loved her sister Shirl too much to play games. We met Billy and his girl later that night and everything was beautiful until we went to a Mr. Big Boys restaurant. They refused to come to our table and take our order, so Billy made a blatant effort to let them know they were prejudice and we left.

We had the time of our lives driving around town going from one party to another. This was also my last night with Shirl for a while because we all had been invited to go to Blythe, California, to pick watermelons and cantaloupes for the summer. I knew that immediately after picking melons I would have to go to Flagstaff to play in the all-star game.

That night I kissed Shirl goodbye for the summer and my heart sunk within me. I didn't know if I could be away from her for three months. I missed her the moment we left her driveway and cried on the inside as we went home to prepare for the trip to Blythe.

With our futures yet hanging in the balance, we went forward but I knew God was on my side. My mother had said so many times in the past, "the Toe is holy ground and anyone who walks there on will be blessed."

They loaded us on a Greyhound bus and took the athletes from Marana and Tucson to Bythe to work in the fields. Every day I wrote Shirl, telling her how much I loved and missed her. She wrote in return, and her letters kept me going.

Now Blythe was worse than the Toe. This was the hottest place in the world. It was one hundred degrees at twelve o'clock midnight. We had rooms which housed four to six people, and we were packed in like sardines. The Toe Boys were housed together, and we were used to being in crowded rooms. They fed us and paid us well, and we all sent the money home.

Man, we were the melon crew. We picked enough melons to supply Arizona and California. They would wake us at three in the morning, and we had to get in the fields because the melons were popping on the vines. Sometimes we worked from sunup to almost midnight.

We would sing and pick melons. The only problem with that job was there were snakes everywhere. I guess they loved the shade of the vines. Every time we would find one we would yell, "Got one!" We would then send him to snake heaven.

DJ and I were talking one day, and I stopped to wipe away the sweat.

DJ yelled, "Codas, a snake!"

I jumped straight up into the air and landed about five feet away from where I was standing. I looked back where I was standing and there was the biggest rattlesnake, about six feet long, squirming on the ground. We tried to find his head so we could kill the snake but his head could not be found. We looked closer and determined that when DJ yelled, I was already standing on the snake's head. When I jumped the weight of my body forced his head into the dirt, and the heel of my shoe smashed his head.

All I could say was, "Thank you, Jesus!"

If I had stepped on his body and not his head I would have been bitten. I thought, *God is yet watching over me!*

Man, we had gotten so good that we could tell if a watermelon or cantaloupe was ripe or not by looking at it. DJ was better at it than any of us. He never brought a bad melon to the room.

In our spare time we had boxing matches using some boxing gloves we had brought for training. There was a kid named Ron who came over to box and watch us, and we all became friends.

We all had been raised up in the church and we decided we had better go to the house of worship one Sunday night. We found a Church of God in Christ, and Cleo, Morris and I were inside enjoying ourselves. Frank and some of the others were outside with the girls. It was embarrassing when the preacher stood up and told the parents to go get their girls, because the boys who were there to work in the fields had bad intentions.

After the girls came back in, so did the boys. Then the pastor asked how many of us loved the Lord, and we all raised our hands. He then said, "If you love the Lord, put a dollar in your hand and wave it at God." So we did as he said and when he saw that we all had money he told all the girls to go get the dollars we were waving at the Lord and bring them to him. That was my last time visiting that particular church.

While working in the fields we met a kid named Dooma-Looma. He was very poor and lived with his grandmother. The Toe Boys did all we could to help this kid and his family. He was always without a shirt and no shoes. We gave him money and food daily, and I prayed daily for his survival. One day hopefully someone from Bythe will tell me that this kid made it in life due to the help of some guys who called themselves the Toe Boys.

We had the times of our lives, and being away from home was what we all needed. I thought about Shirl and going to college. I wanted her to be mine forever. I thought constantly, *Oh God, please make it possible.*

We had made many friends and I met a guy named Ron Z. who seemed to be a nice guy, but a terrible boxer. He would become a friend later in life. When it was time for us to leave, we left with unforgettable memories and a lot of money.

CHAPTER TWENTY-ONE

From Egypt to the Promised Land

My mind was on Shirl, and I anticipated the joy of being with her. I believe that God's peace and serenity for me were personified in her. She had become my heaven on earth; my escape from the pain and suffering that comes from adversities in life. She was my safe place. When I was frustrated with anxieties, her touch would take me to a place in my mind that was out of harm's way. I transcended my environment and found myself in a fresh place with water surrounding me and a cool breeze about me. The air was pure oxygen and each breath penetrated my soul. Her very touch calmed my heart, and tension departed instantly from my body and mind. Sometimes I would be mentally transported to a beach near the ocean or beside a lake filled with clear blue water or a slow-running river that allowed her mist to touch my face and soothe my spirit.

If it was cold and we touched, I transcended to a place of warmth and calmness. It was as if God had wrapped me in a heavenly blanket and laid me on a cloud to rest. My soul and spirit seemed to be saturated with peace and joy, and it warmed me entirely.

When our job was over, the first thing I did when I got home was to make sure my mom was okay. I then went straight to town to see Shirl. When I saw her she looked tired and was very thin. She had spent the summer crying and taking care of her family the best she could. I could see in her face the things she never wrote about in her letters. I embraced her and she would not let me go. I had to convince her that I was real and I was there because I loved her, but how could I tell her I had to go away to the all-star game in a few days? I took her out to dinner and made sure that she ate well. I knew she probably hadn't had a decent meal in a while.

That night we went to a park in the middle of the night and lay down and embraced each other on a bed of grass, under the cover of darkness. Her lips touched mine; our hearts united as one. Our souls melted as the breeze caressed both our bodies. We were one, not just physically joined but soul mates for life. All the time spent with those particular Toe Girls could not equal to a moment with Shirl.

It was the first time we were totally alone. I took her home that night knowing that our relationship would never be the same, for our love went to deeper depths and had soared to a height that we had never ever been before. I felt deep inside that we had cheated ourselves of a precious moment in time.

Shirl's mom was a young hard-working lady. She reminded me of a beautiful flower that faded before its time. I believe in my heart she was the epitome of an abused and used woman. She had lost a set of twins in a miscarriage, and it left her body weak. I don't even know if the other children even knew about this. It was one of those secrets that Shirl had to keep to herself.

I learned to love Lee, which was what we called Shirl's mom. She wanted to be called by her first name, Millie, but I wasn't raised that way. Her middle name was Lee, and you know me, because she insisted that we not call her Mrs. Cook, I called her Lee just to be different.

I think she saw something in Frank and me that she didn't see in Sonny.

She would tell me, "Son, I believe you are real, and I know that Frank loves Mona, but Sonny, he is a charmer, and I haven't quite figured him out yet."

All this time I thought Sonny was pulling the wool over her eyes, but apparently I was wrong. She had figured him out, but she still cared about him as a person. She knew Sonny was about Sonny and no one else.

Lee was young enough to be my mother's daughter. In fact, I had sisters older than her. She was barely old enough to be Shirl's mother. She had been fourteen when Shirl was born. I believe she searched for peace and deliverance in relationships, but could never find it in the men she knew. Truthfully, I think she lowered herself by being with them, and they were not worthy to stand next to her. I think these unworthy and pathetic men could have only dreamed of being with such a woman if it had been another time and another place.

One of them came to me once and confessed that to him she was only a place to stay. I let him know he was talking to the wrong person, because I cared for her. I begin to despise him from that moment on.

Lee was such a beautiful person in the company of so many ugly men. I never told Shirl, but I despised her mother's men friends. I guess men can see through men and women through women. Well, I saw through them, and they were worthless parasitic leeches who could only survive on a living host. They never contributed to her livelihood nor the children they fathered; to me, they were worse than a pathetic infidel.

Lee loved my mother, and I believe she respected her faith more than anything. Mom's faith and her belief in God reached the height of tall mountains and the depth of the oceans.

There were times when I could talk to Lee about things that Shirl could not even relate to. Things like hunting and fishing, working in the cotton fields and the importance of education. I had graduated and Shirl had one more year of high school, and Lee was determined to get all her children through school if it killed her. The adversities of life would one day take their toll and eventually it would cost her life. I knew the boys would make it, but her sisters were questionable, especially Belldurin (that was what we called Deborah) with Sonny. I saw in Deborah a broken heart in the making and a person who would one day become a single parent raising children alone. It was a tragedy in the making, just watching her in this one-sided love affair. I think I was probably the only Toe Boy who actually loved Sonny as a person. I guess I always thought he would grow out of his narcissistic egotistical complex.

I did tell Shirl about having to leave for the all-star game, and it broke her heart. I think Lee consoled her by telling her about the long-term blessings. I didn't have much time to talk to Leroy or Frank. Cleo was trying to get into Eastern Arizona, because that's where Paul and Carl had been. Some of the other Toe Boys had a year or two left in school and the other guys had been taken into the military.

Vietnam was getting stirred up, and the draft was still in. I knew that if I didn't go to college I would go to the military. The Vietnam War was a reality, and it knocked on the door of many of the Toe Boys and they had to answer.

I took a bus to Flagstaff, Arizona, and checked into the dormitory with the other players. They gave us about two weeks to practice before the all-star game. I thought the campus was the most beautiful in the entire world. Everything was green and trees were everywhere. I had never seen so many trees in all my life except for McNary where Pauline lived.

The weather was cool, and I was ready to play. I was from a Class B school and the guys there were mostly Class A through Triple A. One thing the coaches noticed right away was that I was one of the fastest players there. I was easy to be coached, because I had been raised up to respect my elders. I think my politeness touched their heart, but my speed was what caught their attention.

There was a fullback named Herbie who was quite overrated. Herbie was my newly found friend, and he was a good person, but somewhere along life's journey he was told that the sun would rise and set on him. Herbie was an average player to me and was not worthy to tie Leroy's shoelaces, yet he was considered one of the best in Tucson. My talent landed me a spot on offense and defense, and little did I know the new college coach had his eye on me. I knew they were interested because an alumnus of Marana named Tony was asked to talk to me about the school. He really didn't have to say much, because I loved the place.

We practiced long and hard and we even had some time to go to town and look around. My mind was on two things: Shirl and football. I was ready for the game. During our last practice the coaches from Marana came up to support me, and it made me feel great.

We played a hard-fought game, and Herbie was carrying the ball almost every time. It was obvious that they were keying on him, and he couldn't do anything. I thought to myself, *This is dumb coaching.* It seemed that they were more interested in promoting Herbie than winning the game. I was a halfback, and he was the fullback, but I blocked for him most of the game. Somewhere along the way someone woke up and told the coach to give me the ball. I remember the first play I got the ball the game was about over, but I hit the outside like a flash of light. I escaped one player, and after putting a move on a couple more, I slipped to the ground. The people in the stands stood up in amazement. I guess they said, why hasn't this guy carried the ball? Play after play I was able to move the ball, and this opened things up for Herbie as well. We came back from a deficit and won fourteen to seven.

We had friends on both sides of the ball. The team we played against we had become friends with, because we were all from the same state. It was an exciting time of my life, and win or lose, we all won just by being a part of that tradition. I was proud to say I played in the state all-star game.

That night, while in my room, I heard a knock on the door. Tony (the Marana alumni) had brought the coach to see me. That night I knew God had answered my prayers. The coach came in and offered me a full-ride scholarship to attend the college worth a total of eight thousand dollars. This was enough money at that time to cover everything. He didn't even want me to go home, because practice was starting in a week. He thought if I went home he would lose me, so he made me sign a paper saying I intended go to that college. I had to go and see the Toe Boys one last time and to give them the good news.

I got home in time to visit Shirl and give her the good news. She was happy and sad all at the same time.

Lee was happy and said, "Regina has been driving me crazy. I am so glad you're here."

I held Shirl in my arms all night long and thanked God for the moment. That next day I went to the mountain Paul had taken me to when it all started. I went to the summit of that mountain and stood there where the whole world could see me.

I yelled, "I am somebody, I am somebody; I am a child of the King."

I thought about all the hard work Paul had put me through. It had finally paid off. For a moment I thought I saw my father's face in the shape of the clouds smiling at me, but the wind took away the image, and I realized perhaps it was just my imagination. I thought I heard a voice in the wind that said, "This is just the beginning," but again I credited it to my imagination.

The next day I embraced the one woman who taught me that there is nothing too hard for God. I kissed my mama goodbye and savored her last words as she slowly relinquished her embrace. "In all thy ways acknowledge him and he shall direct thy path," she said, as she wiped away a reluctant tear and waved as I left. Her spirit was with me, and I could feel Mama's presence. She was always there.

God works in mysterious ways, and I know he heard my prayers. Cleo came with me and we went up with a friend to Arizona State College, which later became Northern Arizona University.

Sonny later graduated and joined us at N.A.U. We attended school together. Leroy got a scholarship to go to Phoenix College and did for a while. He later went into the military and to N.A.U., and back to the military. At one time Leroy, Cleo, Sonny and I were all at Northern Arizona University together.

Jerry, Cleo's little brother, went to San Diego State. Jerry A, Ed, Morris, Syl, Lee and later Frank went to the military. Frank went to Phoenix College and then to the military where he was decorated with honors and received metals for bravery while in Vietnam. DJ went into the Job Corp and it landed him in the State of Washington, and he became an electrician.

Lloyd, Gootee and Duck went into the Navy. Carl left college and joined the military and spent most of his career in Vietnam. He did so many tours that he started liking Vietnam and combat, so they figured it was time for him to leave.

Paul graduated from the University of Arizona and became rookie of the year for the Cincinnati Bengals. Frank, Sonny and I all planned to marry Shirl, Debbie and Mona. All of the Toe Boys other than Cleo and me went to Vietnam. My prayers again were answered, because not one of them was killed or seriously injured. None fell in battle and though the war touched them deeply, God spared the lives of all the Toe Boys. The Holy Spirit protected them, because they had walked on holy ground in a place called the Toe. God smiled on us and brought us through it all.

I thank God that we were allowed to be children, but as the Apostle Paul once said, "*When I was a child I spoke as a child, I understood as a child, I thought as a child, but when I became a man I put away childish things*" (1Corinthians 13:11, KJV).

We had come to that point in our lives that we were no longer children, and now it was time to be men.

One night, as I lay in my bed in the dormitory and began to reminisce about where I had come from and where I was going, God revealed to me my destiny.

I had always wondered what I must do to be saved from this world of sin, heartaches, and poverty. One night I had a dream that I was on the summit of a mountain. I looked across the world and half of the world was an azure blue. It appeared that the sky was moving towards me. It was as though I was inside a circle and the sky inside the circle was approaching with rapid speed.

While on the summit of that mountain, I asked God, "What must I do to be saved?" and He spoke to me and said, "PREACH!"

As the colored sky came closer, I realized it wasn't the sky at all, but the earth was being covered by a worldwide wave of water. It was so enormous that nothing would escape.

I begin to cry out, "Lord, what I must do to be saved?" Again He said to me, "PREACH THE GOSPEL."

I began to preach to the world from the top of that mountain until I was submerged with water. Again I asked that question, "What I must do to be saved?" and again He said to me, "PREACH! PREACH!"

I began to preach in my mind, because my mouth was shut for fear of swallowing water. I knew that it was only a matter of time when I would let out my breath and breathe in water that surrounded me. I began to anticipate the agony of drowning and the water filling my lungs until death took its hold. I saw around me the boys in the Toe floating dead. I saw family and friends who did not escape the wrath of God. They had refused to accept Christ as their Savior. I could not hold my breath any longer, but before I exhaled I asked the question one more time, "Lord, what must I do to be saved?"

He spoke to me one last time and said, "PREACH! PREACH! PREACH! IF YOU PREACH MY GOSPEL YOU SHALL BE SAVED."

It was then that I released the air that was in my lungs and braced myself for the agony of drowning. Death encompassed me, but to my surprise the air that I breathed was the freshest breath of oxygen I had ever tasted. It was sweet air with the pleasant aroma of flowers that filled my lungs, and my soul was free. The air was pure, clean and refreshing. It was then that I realized that my destiny had been chosen for me, and one day

I would do His Will and preach the Gospel of Jesus Christ that I might live.

My destiny was laid out for me and God would one day call me to his service. I guess Jerry saw it when he had me do the funeral of his friend. Yes, I would one day preach the gospel of Jesus Christ. I will never regret the calling on my life, but I do regret that one day I would have to stand over the casket of those I loved more than life itself and say, "*I heard a voice from heaven saying unto me blessed are the dead who die in the Lord from henceforth. Yea saith the Spirit, that they may rest from their labors, and their works do follow them... earth to earth, ashes to ashes and dust to dust.*"

Each of us in time found that our freedom did not come from leaving the Toe, because in our minds we will always remember and in our hearts there will always be a place for the Toe. We went through trials and tribulations of life, but like the Bible said, "*We are troubled on every side, yet not distressed; we are perplexed, but not in despair; Persecuted, but not forsaken; cast down, but not destroyed*" (2 Corinthians 4:8-9, KJV).

Yes, we went through it all, but even though we had to bend, we did not break. We learned who we were, the power of friendship and the true meaning of brotherly love. It is with great love for God and our parents that we say, thank you. "*For I am persuaded, that neither death, nor life, nor angels, nor principalities, nor powers, nor things present, nor things to come, nor height, nor depth, nor any other creature, shall be able to separate us from the love of God, which is in Christ Jesus our Lord*" (KJV, Romans 8:38-39).

We had all made it to the next level of life, but we could not look forward without first looking back. We thanked God for bringing us through the wilderness, and we were all ready to be led into the Promised Land.

It is that old Negro spiritual that speaks best for all of us and expressed our heartfelt joy, and was so eloquently phrased by Dr. King, "Free at last, free at last, thank God almighty, we're free at last."

The Beginning...